Get
Yourself
ORGANIZED
~ for ~
# CHRISTMAS

Get Yourself ORGANIZED ~for~ CHRISTMAS

Kathi Lipp

HARVEST HOUSE PUBLISHERS
EUGENE, OREGON

Cover by Knail, Salem, Oregon

Cover photo © Nic Taylor / Getty

Published in association with the Books & Such Management, 52 Mission Circle, Suite 122, PMB 170, Santa Rosa, CA 95409-5370, www.booksandsuch.com.

GET YOURSELF ORGANIZED FOR CHRISTMAS
Copyright © 2015 by Kathi Lipp
Published by Harvest House Publishers
Eugene, Oregon 97402
www.harvesthousepublishers.com

Library of Congress Cataloging-in-Publication Data
    Lipp, Kathi, 1967-
    Get yourself organized for Christmas / Kathi Lipp.
       pages cm
    ISBN 978-0-7369-5929-2 (pbk.)
    ISBN 978-0-7369-5930-8 (eBook)
    1. Home economics. 2. Christmas shopping. 3. Christmas decorations. 4. Christmas cooking. 5. Time management. I. Title.
    TX147.L565 2015
    640—dc23

                                                                    2015005627

Printed in the United States of America

          15 16 17 18 19 20 21 22 23 / VP-JH / 10 9 8 7 6 5 4 3 2 1

To Cheri
Thank you for your friendship, partnership,
and teaching me how to be brave.
I am learning to become a better me
by watching you become a better you.

Acknowledgments

Great thanks go to Erin MacPherson, Cheri Gregory, Susy Flory, Renee Swope, Michele Cushatt, and Crystal Paine. So grateful to each and every one of you who kept me together through all of this.

Thanks to Amanda and Shaun, Jeremy, Justen, and Kimberly. We love that we get to celebrate the good stuff with you.

My team: Kim Nowlin, Angela Bouma, Sherri Johnson, Brooke Martinez, and Kimber Hunter.

Rachelle Gardner—you are a gift.

Rod Morris—you rock my world.

To our families: The Richersons, the Lipps, and the Dobsons. Thanks for giving us the best holiday stories.

And finally to Roger. Shut the door, baby.

Contents

The Five-Day Christmas Put Away

Introduction

I think there are two kinds of Christmas extremists.

First, there's your friend who has a selection of ugly Christmas sweaters to choose from for every party. She's the one, first in line, waiting outside of Target on December 26 to stock up on all things Christmas themed. She has formal, semiformal, and casual Christmas dishes. Her husband has submitted film for "The Best Christmas Display" on TLC.

Second, there's your other friend who wants to huddle in the corner where the Christmas tree should have been, rocking back and forth and waiting for January 1 to come.

I hope you fall somewhere in between.

Whether you are filled with magical wonder or dread, one thing is for certain: Ready or not, Christmas is going to happen. And if you're reading this book, my guess is that the thought that Christmas is going to happen fills you with a certain amount of dread.

***

Whether you are filled with magical wonder
or dread, one thing is for certain: Ready
or not, Christmas is going to happen.

I doubt that Christmas is the problem. It's the expectations around Christmas that are killing you.

The shopping, hosting, wrapping, shipping, cooking, designing, decorating, mailing, entertaining, and baking may be things you enjoy. But when there's a time limit, a money limit, and, let's be honest, an energy limit, the things you love can start to turn into things you dread.

And that's why I'm here to help.

You see, I've been there. I was the woman waiting in line at Target, spending twice my annual income, to buy stocking stuffers.

I was the woman who stayed up every night until midnight for a week to bake cookies for a cookie exchange I never wanted to be a part of.

I was the woman who broke down in tears because I ran out of clear tape on Christmas Eve.

And I didn't want to be that woman anymore. In fact, I really didn't like her much.

So I went through a few years of trying to figure out exactly what I wanted my Christmas (and my family's Christmas) to look like.

I wanted to keep the annual viewing of the neighborhood lights (after driving through Starbucks for a Christmas latte,) but ditch the crumbly cookie exchange.

I wanted to read the Christmas story, but not feel obligated to tell our story in a Christmas letter every single year.

I wanted to have some time just with my husband to celebrate the holiday, instead of making him wait until December 31 to reconnect with his wife.

And I want you to have the kind of Christmas you love.

I want you to have the kind of Christmas where you celebrate the things that are truly important to you: faith, family, friends. (And, for me, throw in a little fun and food, and you've got yourself a truly magical holiday.)

> ✳ ✳ ✳
>
> I want you to have the kind of Christmas
> where you celebrate the things that are truly
> important to you: faith, family, friends.

I want you to put aside the expectations of what you "should do" and truly dig into what you want to do this Christmas season.

And let's be clear: this isn't about one day. I don't want you to just get to *the* day and then collapse in exhaustion. I want you to have joy, peace, and a plan for the whole holiday season.

I think having an organized Christmas is important. But what I really want for you is to have a Christmas that is clutter free. Free of emotional, physical, and relational clutter.

So as we together work our way through the 21 projects in this book, I will be giving you tips to keep down the clutter in your Christmas.

When I asked my friends what a clutter-free Christmas would look like, here is one of my favorite responses. Fellow author Jill Davis was forced to look at every area of her holiday celebration after her life took a decidedly different direction:

> When I got divorced eight years ago and had to make huge changes in life with my four children, I asked them what was most important to them. We chose two traditions—the advent calendar and sugar cookies, plus their favorite gifts of pajamas and a book on Christmas Eve. So much easier than all the shopping, baking, cleaning, and decorating I used to do. Instead of having a beautifully decorated home, fabulous things to eat, lots of Christmas presents, and a frantic mom, they now have an easygoing, low-key, lightly

decorated Christmas with a very present mom. Life is better. Christmas is easier. We are all happier.

A clutter-free Christmas says that we are doing only those things that are truly important. We are not getting weighed down by unnecessary expenditures, obligations, or craziness.

* * *

A clutter-free Christmas says that we are doing only those things that are truly important.

Throughout the book, I'm going to offer some ideas on how to make it a clutter-free Christmas—one that everyone can enjoy. And maybe for the first time this December, you will truly experience a little Peace on Earth.

A Brief Word About the Projects

You may be picking this book up on October 5. Good for you. You have a head start on all the projects.

Or maybe your best friend just pressed this book into your hand on December 9. OK. Take a deep breath. You can double up on some of the projects, and then store this book with your fall decorations so you're ahead of the game for next year.

Whenever you begin (and if you have a choice, I would aim to start around the beginning or middle of November), I promise you'll make it through.

If you're getting a late start, it's even more important to do only the things that truly need to be done. In other words, skip the Christmas letter but save the Christmas fudge. We all must have our priorities straight.

Whenever you start, I suggest you first read through all the projects. There may be some you can skip this year. And remember, you have a few catch-up days to do the things that need to get done. Don't worry. You've got this.

Four Steps to Kick Off Your Christmas Right

Expectations.

If there is anything that can make your Christmas a holiday to dread, it is expectations.

Others' expectations.

Expectations of how things should be.

Your expectations of yourself.

A year is a long time between celebrations. In that time, you may have forgotten certain things. Like, how no one in the family ate any of your cranberry cheese mold (the one that took up an entire shelf in your fridge for five hours). Or how everyone loved it when you showed the JibJab video of your family with "Rockin' Around the Christmas Tree." And they can't wait to see what video you are showing this year.

So I say, deal with those expectations right up front.

First, find out what's important to the family or close friends you celebrate Christmas with.

One year, after being exhausted by all the demands for different types of food each of my kids had told me we *had* to have, I finally asked them, "Tell me what's truly important to you."

Their answer? Pumpkin cheesecake.

That's what was important to everyone. The no-bake cheesecake that Roger makes every year. That was the deepest desire of my kids' hearts.

* * *

The no-bake cheesecake that Roger
makes every year—that was the
deepest desire of my kids' hearts.

So this time, I didn't make a huge selection of every food that we've ever enjoyed. We made the meal, had some family favorites, and made the cheesecake.

It was simple, and everyone was happy.

Second, figure out what's important to you.

When we're in charge of making Christmas miracles, we are so busy creating the Christmas that everyone else wants, we forget to step back and look at what's important and meaningful to us.

I want you to imagine for a moment not the perfect Christmas, but what you want Christmas to feel like. Peaceful? Joyous? Comfortable? Figure out what's important to you, and then plan toward that.

* * *

When we're in charge of making Christmas
miracles, we are so busy creating the
Christmas that everyone else wants, we
forget to step back and look at what's
important and meaningful to us.

If you want a peaceful Christmas, but you're still making sixteen different kinds of cookies (and you lost your love of baking right after the snickerdoodles and the fudgy fantastic flourless cookies), then your plan is at odds with what's important to you.

Third, gather your Christmas stash.

Gather all your Christmas supplies into their appointed areas, such as your wrapping paper, gift bags, ribbon, tape, tissue, and so on. This will keep you from constantly being surprised about what you have, and more importantly, what you don't. Make a list of everything you need to buy.

Fourth, make a list of how others can help.

Last year, I made an amazing discovery about my husband. He is not in the least offended when I tell him what to do. In fact, he appreciates it.

I made this discovery when we were both waiting for our coffee to brew. As I was waiting, I was unloading the dishwasher, wiping down the counters, and refilling the water bowl for the dog.

And Roger? He was standing there.

At first I was a little irritated. How could he just stand there while I was working? Shouldn't he want to help?

So I asked him, "Hey, could you put away the silverware?"

And he said "Sure!"

We discussed it later, and I found out he honestly didn't notice that anything needed to be done. "I'm always willing to do this stuff," he said, "but sometimes I just don't think of it."

So now, after dinner, we have a new ritual. Roger does dishes, my least favorite part of kitchen cleanup. With dishes, it's straightforward and there aren't a lot of decisions to be made. And while he's doing dishes, I'm putting food away, taking the dirty towels to the laundry, wiping down counters, and so on.

The difference? I see what needs to be done.

And that's a lot like Christmas. You probably have a natural instinct about what needs to be done for Christmas. Others in your family? Not so much.

My husband is always happy to help. But when it comes to Christmas, he needs a little direction.

* * *

You probably have a natural instinct about
what needs to be done for Christmas.
Others in your family? Not so much.

Every year we have people over for our celebration, and the most common question is, "How can I help?" (I invite only nice people over.) In the heat of the moment (and in the heat of the kitchen), I'm almost always at a loss for how to direct people on how to assist.

So this year, I did something different. As I made my check-lists of Christmas prep (for the season) and meal and party prep (for the day), I highlighted anything that someone else could do.

So when guests asked in advance, "What can I bring?" or "Is there any way I can help?," I was able to look at my list and say, "Yep—could you pick up ice on your way here?" Or, "We're short on appetizers. I would love for you to bring your famous cheese puffs!"

And on the day of the event, when people wandered into the kitchen and asked, "How can I help?" I was able to look at my list and say, "You can chop the celery for the stuffing," or "I would love for you to put out the cheese-and-cracker plate. Here's everything you'll need."

By spending fifteen extra minutes thinking through what others can do, you're going to save yourself not only time but also wear and tear.

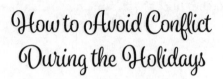

How to Avoid Conflict During the Holidays

A SURVIVOR'S GUIDE

Is it possible to avoid conflict during the holidays?

Probably not completely. But the time to start thinking about it is now—not when you feel like threatening your husband with a spontaneous trip to your mom's house because you just can't stand his mom anymore.

All of these strategies, bathed in prayer and a whole lot of grace (and some dark chocolate thrown in for good measure), will help this be the most peaceful holiday season since the time you and your husband got snowed in and couldn't travel to be with family.

Have the Conflict Early

Most families experience conflict during the holidays because they tried to avoid conflict earlier on. We hope that things will "just work out" and that everyone will "just be cool." If there's a hard conversation that needs to be had about how your father-in-law talks to your kids, or how much your adult daughter drinks at the family gathering, the time to have those hard conversations is December 5, not December 25.

> ***
> Most families experience conflict
> during the holidays because they
> tried to avoid conflict earlier on.

Take the "Plans" Approach

My stepdaughter, Amanda, just got engaged this week. We could not be more thrilled, and it's kind of hard to contain our excitement about planning. So when she called me to talk wedding plans, I said, "Hey, if you don't want to get together and talk weddings, I totally understand. You've got a lot of people you're trying to please."

Then she told me something that made me burst with pride. "Actually, I'm doing the same thing you and Dad do. I'm saying, 'Here are the plans I've made. If you're able to join us for _____, that's great. If not, we totally understand.'" She said that giving people a choice has taken so much of the pressure off of trying to make everyone happy.

I love it. She is behaving in a healthy way, not giving her control over to other people and not feeling like she needs to control others either.

Know the Rule of Three

In engineering, there is an old saying: "You can have it better, cheaper, and faster. Pick two out of three." And it's true. How could you have a product delivered with better quality, made cheaper, and ahead of schedule? It might be possible, but you'll kill the engineer in the process.

Roger and I have adopted a similar motto for family celebrations: "You can celebrate on the traditional day, you can have the whole family together, or you can have people be happy about it. Pick two out of three."

***

You can celebrate on the right day, you can have the whole family together, or you can have people be happy about it. Pick two out of three.

With blended families and in-law relationships (or even if your son is just dating a girl!), holidays put stress not only on you and your husband but on your kids as well. They are charged with keeping loyalties, keeping the peace, and keeping things from blowing up.

We realized early on in our marriage that two things were important: Having everyone together, and having everyone be as happy as possible about it. The date? That really didn't matter to either of us. Often, we celebrate on a date other than the actual holiday. We're having Thanksgiving on Thanksgiving Day this year, but we're celebrating Christmas on the twenty-sixth when all the kids can be here. On the twenty-fifth? Church and then jammies all day.

Budget

If money is one of your biggest stressors, then the weeks leading up to Christmas are the hot-zone times for conflict. Come up with your budget now so that everyone's expectations will line up.

Ask

Ask your family what traditions are important and which ones have run their course. Do all of your kids love the Starbucks-and-Christmas-light night, but they're over the matching pajamas on Christmas morning? Kill the pj's and keep the lights.

Your Projects for a
Clutter-Free Christmas

What's Your Christmas Plan?

It is my sincere hope that no one feels like a failure around Christmastime. But I've felt that way myself, way too many times to count.

I think of all those times I started dreaming about Christmas in late October or early November and thought everything was possible. I was going to throw the parties, make the meals, send the cards, arrange the cookie exchanges, and generally be awesome at Christmas. I was going to rule this holiday.

But my vague notions of what Christmas should look like rarely translated into the Festival of Awesomeness that I'd imagined. Because sadly, the world doesn't take a break for Christmas. Time to prep and plan? Nobody is getting any time off to plan the perfect Christmas.

***

My vague notions of what Christmas should look like rarely translated into the Festival of Awesomeness that I'd imagined.

So what's a body to do? Just try your best to have a good Christmas and figure it out as you go?

I think the key is to take a few minutes, step back, and really think about what is important to you. Instead of engaging in crisis control the entire Christmas season, you can actually go in with a plan—not so much about what you want to do but what you don't need to worry about.

But before you can come up with the list of what you will and won't do, you need to come up with a clear idea of what is truly important to you.

Start planning now, and you will experience a more sacred and sane holiday this year. Promise!

✳ **Project 1:** Create Your Holiday Mission Statement ✳

Here is what you will need:

* ✳ two or three index cards
* ✳ a marker
* ✳ My Holiday Mission Statement form (available at the back of the book)

I know, I know. You want to dive in and start checking things off your list since it's going to be a busy few weeks. I get it. But first I want you to spend ten minutes determining this: *What do you want your Christmas to look like this year?*

If we can go into the holidays being intentional about how we spend our time and our physical and emotional energy, it truly will be the key to a more sane and sacred celebration.

✳ ✳ ✳

Being intentional about how we spend our time and our physical and emotional energy is the key to a more sane and sacred celebration.

On the Holiday Mission Statement, I want you to spend some time looking at what you want your season of celebration to look like. Here are some words that might spark some thoughts:

time	patience	activities
energy	gift giving	include
priorities	commitment	God
spiritual	community	restore
friends	charity	food
family	church	peace
travel	reflect	joy
focus	honor	self-control
celebrate	provide	serve
growth	creativity	together
tradition	love	connect
creating	cherish	care

Brainstorm about what is important to you. Some years, I'm looking for joy. I want to experience that deep, abiding joy that only comes from God and being with His people.

In 2011, it was different: I was all about peace. Between chaos in my ministry, chaos in our home lives, chaos in my husband's job, and a triple shot of chaos with my mom's health, I needed that peace that passes understanding. Here is what my mission statement looked like for Christmas 2011:

> *I will share God's peace with my family, my friends, and people I meet, and I will be done with my prep by December 20 so that I can experience peace during our celebration. I will read the Christmas story each morning of December.*

And yes, God delivered that—even while at the mall. In December.

In 2012, here is what I wanted my Christmas to look like:

During this Christmas season, I want to throw off any old traditions that are just habits and do those things that:

1. *Bring me closer to God*

2. *Bring us together as a family*

3. *Equip us to serve*

* * *

Once you know what is important to you, you can figure out how you're going to get there.

Once you know what is important to you, you can figure out how you're going to get there. And here's where those index cards and marker come in handy. This is what I wrote:

I will ask in advance for help from my family (spouse, parents, sibling, kids).

In order to remind myself (and those I love) about this Christmas plan, I'm putting it on an index card in three places:

- *On the fridge*

- *On my computer*

- *On the visor of my car*

(And yes, these are the three places that I need a little more Jesus during the holidays.)

I've been doing a Holiday Mission Statement since 2011, and it has made a huge change in how I approach the holidays.

***

Doing a Holiday Mission Statement has made a huge change in how I approach the holidays.

This past year, my Holiday Mission was simple. I wanted to experience joy in the midst of sorrow. My dad passed away September 5. We were all still processing the loss and what that looked like to our family.

But there were some real opportunities for joy—sharing memories, eating some of his favorite foods, and loving on each other. We kept the celebration easy (celebrating on the 26, only three gifts for each of our kids, and a Secret Santa gift exchange for our extended family). While it was nothing that HGTV would feature in an *Elegant Extravagance Holiday Special*, it was perfect for our family and the place we were in. We gave ourselves a pass on anything that wasn't necessary, and we just loved on each other, played games, went to church, and remembered what was special in our lives. It was, I dare say, the perfect Christmas.

Make It a Clutter-Free Christmas

Now that you've decided what you want your Christmas to look like, it is important that you don't let all the holiday madness sneak back in. You get to decide exactly how crazy this season is. If you truly want to have a clutter-free Christmas, it starts with how you spend your time, energy, and money. When you stick to your Christmas mission, you are saying that the world doesn't get a say in how you celebrate.

* * *

When you stick to your Christmas
mission, you are saying that the world
doesn't get a say in how you celebrate.

Kathi's Quick Tips

* If you're having a hard time coming up with your mission statement, step back for a day and think on it. This mission is not to add stress to your life—it's to focus you for the season so you can truly bless others and receive the blessings.

* Still stuck? Maybe you're stuck trying to make it the "perfect" Holiday Mission. If that's the case, aim for 80 percent. Get most of your mission statement down on paper, and give yourself permission to go back and change about 20 percent later on. It's your mission statement. You get to decide how it goes.

What kind of Christmas do you want—or maybe need—this year? Step back, think about it, and plan for it now.

Put Together Your Christmas Binder

When I was in the seventh grade, I saved all my babysitting money to buy, not a pair of Keds or a Tiffany CD but four Trapper Keeper binders. Yes, four. One for school, one to keep track of my babysitting jobs, one for notes and such, and the last one, well, just in case one of the other ones broke or went missing.

Now you may be thinking that I was a bit geeky. Who chooses an office product over new shoes? But in reality, it was pure brilliance.

> ***
>
> The first step to any great project is getting
> your thoughts together and all in one place.

When you have all your stuff in one place, you can easily keep track of it. And seventh-grade Kathi seemed to innately know what I now know for a fact: The first step to any great project is getting your thoughts together and all in one place.

And today's project does just that—gets your Christmas all in one place. So you can be organized and ready for whatever the season throws at you.

✳ **Project 2**: Put Together Your Christmas Binder ✳

Today, I want you to create a safe place to keep all your Christmas stuff.

If you're like most people, you have your recipes in various cookbooks, a bunch of envelopes from last year's Christmas cards stuffed into a kitchen drawer, and your Christmas stamps attached to your fridge with a magnet.

Stop the madness.

I want you to grab a binder (yes, you can go buy a bona fide Trapper Keeper at Target, or you can scavenge one from your kid's room) and start pulling all your loose papers, Christmas labels, lists, and recipes and any other holiday-related paraphernalia into one place.

Here is what you will need:

* ✳ binder
* ✳ binder tabs
* ✳ sheet protectors
* ✳ three-hole punch
* ✳ permanent marker

If you don't have all these items lying around the house, no worries. The important thing is to gather all your holiday-related papers into one place. Even if you have just a file folder lying around, that will do for now.

If you do have the binder and the tabs, here are some sections of the binder you may want to consider (you don't have to use them all; in fact, the simpler the better):

* ✳ Calendar
* ✳ Christmas Cards

* Recipes
* Hiding Places
* Christmas Gift Lists
* Menus
* Receipts (use a page protector to store these in that section)
* Budget
* To-Do List

Start sorting all your gathered papers into a sheet protector in the appropriate section. When you have everything Christmas-related in one place, it's going to make it a lot easier to find your favorite pumpkin custard recipe or the receipt for the Barbie toothbrush that your daughter just said "is for babies" and needs to go back to the store.

Make It a Clutter-Free Christmas

* This is probably your first year keeping a Christmas Binder. It's probably a nice, thin binder that is totally manageable. But as the years go on, you are going to be throwing a lot of things into that binder. Make sure at the beginning of every holiday season that you clear out everything you won't need: old envelopes, leftover Christmas cards, and Pinterest ideas that looked fun in the moment, but you know will never see the light of day.

* While putting together your binder, add only those things that you will really use. One of the secrets of keeping the binder usable is to keep it uncluttered.

Kathi's Quick Tips

* Make sure to spend a few minutes updating your binder every day. Remember what happened in school when you kept sliding things in there without putting them in the rings?

* If you want a fun cover for your binder (which, I admit, I always do), I made one for you! Head to ChristmasProject.org to download a free printable PDF.

* Some people like digital binders—and if that's you, I get it. Sort of. But I also think that digital lacks the capability to store receipts, grab jotted notes, tear out recipes, and so on. So if you're a digital person, go for it. But make sure you have a folder where you can stash things until you have a chance to scan them.

* When Christmas is over, store your binder for next year as is. You may end up throwing out some of the stuff, but you'll already have a good start on next year's binder.

Pick Your Christmas Card Picture

I have mixed feelings about getting Christmas cards and letters.

The ones from good friends with pictures of cute couple, kids and dog, and sweet notes about what's been going on the past year? Adore.

The ones with the detailed list of accomplishments and how everyone in the family is a genius and the middle-school son is on his way to a career in the NFL? Pass.

I love some humor, some highlights, and some truth. That's the kind of Christmas card and letter I want to get.

Let me be the first to say that I don't think sending a Christmas card is a requirement for being a good mom, wife, daughter, or friend. I have several people in my life I've never received a card from, and I don't think any less of them and know that I'm loved.

That being said, I do love receiving those cards and pictures. If you are one of my friends who sends them, thanks.

And I don't always send them. No cards went out the year I had a book due, my mom had cancer, and I had whooping cough all in the same two-week span. If you are having that kind of holiday season, you get a Christmas card pass. If you'd like, I can even write you a note (like the ones your mom wrote to get you out of gym class when you were feeling not your best).

> * * *
>
> No cards went out the year I had a book
> due, my mom had cancer, and I had
> whooping cough all in the same two-week
> span. If you are having that kind of holiday
> season, you get a Christmas card pass.

So, if you've decided not to do a card this year, go do something fun like watch *Elf* or have a cup of cocoa with a friend. For the rest of you, you have a job to do. But it's a fun one: Today, I want you to pick the picture that's going to go on your card.

* **Project 3**: Pick Your Christmas Card Picture *

You actually have a choice of assignments today. You can either:

* Pick your Christmas picture (if you're including one in your cards) or
* Set a date to take a family picture.

See? Fun and easy. If you already have the photo on your phone, computer, or in your iPhoto account, you can send it to Costco, Target, or your card company to get it ready for your cards. But for today, just enjoy looking through all those pics on your computer (or your phone) and remembering how blessed you and yours have been this year.

> *** *
>
> For today, just enjoy looking through all those
> pics on your computer and remembering how
> blessed you and yours have been this year.

What kind of photo do you want? Professional, a candid snapshot, something you found from this summer? Anything goes when it comes to today's Christmas cards.

Make It a Clutter-Free Christmas

Our Christmas photos are always less than perfect. Last year we had no decent pics of our whole family together, so we just did a collage. A couple of years ago we had an adorable picture of our whole family in the snow—except my daughter Kimber was holding an ice scraper. I thought about Photoshopping it out or not using the picture, but every time I see that picture, I remember that it snowed so much in Lake Tahoe that we almost got snowed in. And just as we were digging out our cars, my brother gathered us all together to take that picture. I love it for all the memories it has for me.

That is what I call a "perfect" picture. Ice scraper and all.

Kathi's Quick Tips

I asked my readers their best suggestions for getting great family shots. Here are some been-there-done-that ideas:

Everyone SMILE!

> "Let yourself *and* your husband and kiddos be *themselves*. The photos you like will be the photos that were taken during interaction moments—not with

everyone smiling for the camera. If you let the photographer do their job, you may catch moments between your family members that you never would have imagined."—Jamie

"We have three young kids, and our favorite local photographer is our only hope of getting at least one great shot. She is amazing with kids and tells plenty of jokes to get real smiles out of my kids. We bribe them with treats, and we always take pictures outside where they can play and roam a bit. We try to have a fun dinner and family time after."—Amber

Location, Location, Location

"Choose a location that has some meaning to you—a park you love, grandpa's backyard, the place you took your engagement photos. Having some history in your setting adds a nice dimension to your photos."—Jodie

"Take the same shot in the same place every year, preferably a favorite spot. It's a beautiful way to chronicle your family's growth and change. We take ours on a fav beach spot."—Tracey

Dressing the Part

"We make it fun. It's always thematic and most years that includes costumes. And by thematic I mean characters from a movie or superheroes."—Bronwyn

"Plan clothes ahead of time to coordinate the colors and then choose a location to suit the look you're going for."—Tabitha

Photo Hacks

> "Get a photobook made with your 'last twelve months' photo file. I make them as gifts for grandparents and get one for us as well. Walgreens is reasonably priced and does a good job. You can order several book styles, add text captions, and have your year at a glance!"—Tracey

> "I'm going to try this this year with my teenage boys—find an old picture of them and try to get as close to that picture as possible. Then I'll put those photos side by side on a Christmas card."—Becky

Hiring a Photographer

> "My family hired a photographer to take family pictures. If you do this, make sure you get a photographer who is patient with kids. Ours wasn't and was very short with my grandchildren and my nephew who has Asperger's syndrome. Personally, I prefer to take candid and family planned/setup shots."—Cheryl

If you do hire a photographer, here are some hints from the real deal. Mollie Burpo is the owner of Bloom Photography in Austin, Texas (www.bloomaustin.com), and no one gets better expressions out of kids than Mollie. Here are her super-secret insider tips for getting the most out of your professional session with your family.

1. Plan Ahead

Don't leave family photography to the last minute. Love a pro photo from a friend's Christmas card? Ask her who took it and bookmark the photographer's site. Adore a friend's Facebook profile picture? Fan the photographer on Facebook and see whose images really connect with you over the course of the year. Most photographers' calendars fill up early in this very busy portrait season, so start looking for fall specials or reserve your date when summer is starting to wrap up, long before the cool weather hits. Be sure to choose a photographer based on the way their images make you feel.

> ** * **
>
> Most photographers' calendars fill up early, so look for fall specials or reserve your date when summer is wrapping up.

2. Time and Location

Is your family full of morning people or night owls? Does your little one perk up following their afternoon nap? The best light for outdoor photography is typically in the early morning or late afternoon, so pick a time that sets you up for the most success. Be sure to plan for snacks. Full bellies equal the best smiles! Also, think ahead about a location where your kids will be comfortable and safe and even have fun. Avoid parks with playgrounds that will distract and tempt your kiddos unless you are happy doing the photo session on the swings.

> ** * **
>
> Think about a location where your kids will be comfortable and safe and even have fun.

3. All Dressed Up

As moms, let's be honest—our kids look cute in every single thing they wear. We are much pickier about our own best looks. For this reason, I highly suggest moms start with dressing themselves. Choose something flattering and comfortable that makes you feel confident and beautiful. Then choose the children's and husband's outfits to coordinate. I always plan by choosing a pattern for my husband or kids with multiple colors—a plaid or stripes works great—and pull solids and other patterns including those colors into everyone else's attire. You can never miss with neutrals and a pop of rich jewel tone color.

Don't leave this step to the last minute. You will add to the stress of the experience if you are running from store to store the morning of your session. Start planning the attire a minimum of three weeks in advance to allow for shipping and returns or exchanges.

4. Relax

You have hired a professional—let them do their job. Just as the teacher is in charge in the classroom, this is the photographer's domain.

* * *

You have hired a professional—
let them do their job.

The best thing you can do as a parent is relax and focus on enjoying your family. Don't coach, threaten, or lecture your kids. If you are offering an incentive for good behavior (a treat or privilege), let the photographer know, and they can gently remind your kids if necessary.

PROJECT 4

Prep Your Christmas Card

Remember, you are no less of a Christmas elf if you end up not sending Christmas cards. In fact, try this little experiment:

Sit back, close your eyes, and tell yourself, "I'm not sending Christmas cards this year!"

How did that make you feel?

Sad?

Relieved?

If you are leaning toward relieved, would you consider, seriously, not sending them out? Maybe next year you'll actually look forward to it.

However, if you are going to send them out, there are a few steps you need to take:

1. Pick your Christmas cards.

2. Gather up mailing addresses.

3. Organize addresses.

4. Print addresses.

5. Get stamps.

6. Get your return address stamp, stickers, or have it printed on the envelopes.

No wonder so many of us quit in the middle.

So today, all I want you to do is create a folder on your computer, select your Christmas cards, gather the addresses you plan on sending cards to, and order or pick up your stamps.

*** *** ***

Next Christmas, you will find your
binder, open this computer folder, and
you'll have everything you need.

The first thing I want you to do is create a folder on your computer called "Christmas." This is where everything for your Christmas celebration will go that you need to store on your computer. Next Christmas, you will find your binder, open this computer folder, and you'll have everything you need for your Christmas.

Addresses

For addresses, get any envelopes and lists from last year, your address book, and your online address book. Create an Excel spreadsheet with all the info you will need. (You'll be super grateful next year when you don't have to hand write all those addresses again.)

Create your list. This may take a couple of sessions, but no fear, I've put a couple of work sessions into these projects! Once you get your list together, you'll be able to either hand address your envelopes or create a Mail Merge from your Excel list. You can find a great tutorial on "How to Create a Mail Merge" at www.gcflea rnfree.org/word2013/31/print. It will take a time or two to learn, but it's a great skill to have. And if you want to make labels and Mail Merge scares you, ask a friend for help—and then bake some cookies for her.

Pick a Card, Any Card

As far as cards go, all you have to do is make your decision between custom cards or store bought. Yes, custom are cute. Store bought are great for those who might be late getting started.

Order Stamps

Don't wait to get your stamps until the week before and then have to wait in line at the post office. You can have stamps delivered to your mailbox by going through USPS.com. Order the theme you want, pay online, and have them waiting for you when your cards are ready to go!

Make It a Clutter-Free Christmas

* Two Christmases ago, I took all my leftover Christmas cards and sent those out instead of buying new ones. I put in a simple letter with an update on our family and sent them on their way. Did anyone notice that they got the same card from us two years in a row? Maybe, though probably not. But who cares? I used up a bunch of cards and saved some cash. Plus, I still had leftovers after that, which I used as gift tags.

* Cull your Christmas card list. Just because you sent a card to someone you cared about twelve years ago doesn't mean you have to send them a card for the rest of your life. One friend does a big blowout card to everyone on their list every five years, and then sends cards just to close friends and family the other years.

* If you are one of those women who said she wanted a simpler Christmas, may I politely suggest an adorable, standard-sized, store-bought card? (And if you're making your cards from scratch, I can't even talk to you.)

Kathi's Quick Tips

* Make sure to hang on to any cards that are returned because of a wrong address and update your address

file on your computer. So much better than sending
to the wrong address five years in a row.

* Put your stamps in your Christmas Binder. How
many times have I put my stamps some place safe only
to find them January 5.

"Kathi, *I did it!* I picked my photo and ordered my cards. I cannot thank you enough for your Christmas Project. I have *never* had my Christmas cards ordered this early. In addition to picking my photo, I actually organized my photos on iPhoto. So I completed two tasks in one. Woo-hoo! Thanks for your help. I'm actually excited this year about Christmas!"

Shari

Schedule Your Time for the Holidays

OK, it's time to kick the Christmas plans into high gear. Spend fifteen minutes scheduling out all your commitments for the next few weeks on a blank calendar.

> ***
>
> It's so easy to have great ideas and let them all slip through your fingers because of the craziness of the season.

It's so easy to have great ideas ("Let's go look at Christmas lights!" "Let's curl up and watch *Elf* one night this week!") and let them all slip through your fingers because of the craziness of the season. So along with all the chores of the season, let's schedule in some fun!

* **Project 5**: Schedule Your Time for the Holidays *

Here is what you will need:

* * a blank calendar for November and December
* * school calendars, church calendars, work and personal calendars

Head on over to my ChristmasProject.org page and download printable blank calendars for November and December. After you've filled them out, put them on your fridge so everyone knows the holiday plans. Here are some things you may want to consider with your schedule:

* kids' school calendar
* work events
* church events
* parties and other fun

Once you've filled in all the already-scheduled activities, set aside some pockets of time to work on prepping for Christmas. Here are some things you may want to schedule some time for:

* get tree
* cookie baking
* decorating
* project nights (for wrapping, card addressing, ordering gifts online)
* a night to go look at Christmas lights
* a night to watch *It's a Wonderful Life*

Make It a Clutter-Free Christmas

I'm not saying you should do all of those things (in fact, I don't think you should), but if you want to do any of these or any other family or friend activities, put them on your calendar so you can plan around them. And make sure the rest of your family and friends can see the schedule as well.

Try taking one activity off your calendar that you "always" do but may have lost some of its meaning. I used to do an advent calendar every year. It was big and cute and had twenty-four pockets at the bottom, each holding a wrapped ornament for my kids to take turns placing on the big felt tree.

***

Try taking one activity off your calendar that you "always" do but may have lost some of its meaning.

One year I brought it out, hung it up, and announced to my eleven-year-old, Justen, that it was his turn to unwrap the advent surprise. "Is there money in there?" he asked. Um, no... "OK, then just let Kimmy do it."

I was crushed.

Truth was, Justen didn't care about the advent calendar, and after a couple of years, neither did Kimberly. Yes, we still celebrated advent. But they were past the age of wanting to unwrap knick-knacks every morning for a month.

I wrapped up the advent tree and put it away, a little sad, but also realizing that it still had a future. Seven years later my brother had a daughter, Elsa, who now does the advent tree. Someday Elsa will outgrow it, probably about the time that my kids start having kids, and the tradition can continue.

Kathi's Quick Tips

* Limit the number of kid activities each of your children are participating in. Lots of excitement mixed with equal parts sugar can wreak havoc with your schedule.

* Make sure you have a couple at-home nights every
  week to just be with your people. You will need some
  downtime to really enjoy the rest of the week without
  feeling frantic.

When you're snuggled up on the couch with your family, eating fresh-baked cookies while watching *It's a Wonderful Life*, you'll thank me.

Get Your Gift List Together

My daughter, Kimber, has gift-giving anxiety. Actually, for her it's more like gift-receiving anxiety.

Kim is a sensitive girl and hates the thought of hurting anyone's feelings. She also is a terrible liar, which, when she was a teenager, was a blessing for this mom. As a gift receiver? It's a huge handicap.

As we'd all gather around the tree to open gifts, grandparents would wait anxiously to see the look of delight on Kim's face as she opened the scarf they'd bought her or the notebook she'd described wanting.

But Kimber is not one for whom any old scarf will do. It needs to be the exact scarf she saw at H&M or the notebook with the college-ruled paper and the black cover. So when her honest reaction was less than utter joy, Kimber felt on the spot and judged.

> * * *
> To give a gift that my daughter truly
> wants is a wonderful thing.

We've eliminated all that now. She gives me a list of links to the things she actually wants. You would think that would eliminate the Christmas magic. It does not. To give a gift that my daughter truly wants is a wonderful thing. I am not about surprise, but I am all about delight.

✳ **Project 6:** Get Your Gift List Together ✳

For this project, write out all your gift ideas and what gifts you've already bought. You can print out lists to keep in your Christmas Binder over at ChristmasProject.org.

Wouldn't it be great if the gift-giving part of Christmas was the least stressful? Here are a couple ideas to help you take the stress off:

Limit the List

For several years, we limited the number of gifts we bought for each kid: one spiritual gift, one clothing gift, and one fun gift. You may think that sounds very *Little House on the Prairie*-ish, but with all the grandparents, aunts and uncles, and friends, the kids weren't hurting for gifts. Trust me. We plan to limit gifts again this year now that all the kids are adults and bringing other people into the family (through marriage).

Extended Family Swap

We're doing this with my extended family this year. We used Elfster.com, and my stepdaughter, Amanda, registered all of us through Facebook. You can be registered through an email address as well. The website automatically assigns you a person, and then that person can make gift suggestions and put links to the items on Amazon or other online retailers. This is especially helpful if the person assigned to you is someone you don't spend every day with or, if they're like Kimber, only one shade of lipstick will do. Having the link to a website where I can order the correct shade? Priceless.

***

If a family gift swap is something you
want to try, talk about it with your family
now, not the week of Christmas.

Every time I start to panic about not having a gift for my brother, I stop, take a deep breath, and remember—"He's not on my list this year." Huzzah. If this is something you want to try, talk about it with your family now, not the week of Christmas.

Ask

Ask people what they would like. I know it's fun to surprise people with something perfect, but really, why stress yourself out?

Keep Your Ears Open

Print out the Gift List over at ChristmasProject.org and start to take notes for each person you're buying for. Maybe your son mentioned a book he's interested in or your husband received a renewal notice for his favorite magazine. Make a quick note to get it or jot it down for next year.

Stalk Them on Social Media

Some of my best gift ideas this past year came from things my family posted on social media. My daughter talked about a cookie she was obsessed with, and my son put a link to some *Star Wars* posters he was in love with. With both of them being broke, I knew neither of them would be purchasing those items for themselves, so they made great Christmas gifts.

* * *

Some of my best gift ideas came from things my family posted on social media.

Give to Charity

One thing we love to do is give a charitable gift in the name of those friends and relatives who always say, "Don't buy me anything. I already have too much stuff!" Here are some ideas of ways to honor someone through a charitable gift:

* If they are an animal lover, give to a local animal shelter.

* If they love kids, how about a children's charity, such as Compassion International.

* A local food bank is always a great option for a contribution. Think about making the donation in the town where they grew up.

Make It a Clutter-Free Christmas

Try to limit your list. I'm not saying kick people off completely, but think outside the wrapped Christmas box for some other ideas:

* If you know that someone in your family or group is struggling financially, could you suggest that you all take a year's reprieve from gift giving? There's nothing worse (I know from personal experience) than being the broke one in the family and having to come up with Christmas miracles for everyone.

* When my kids were younger, they had more time than money and would give their grandparents the gift of several hours of chores around the house. Instead of giving my parents another knickknack they didn't need, my daughter gave them six hours of garage and housecleaning. Not only did my mom love the

help, she loved the time she got to spend with her granddaughter.

* For large groups that might be tempted to exchange gifts, what if you went out for lunch instead? No one feels left out, and you all get to enjoy each other's company. Double win.

* What if, instead of physical gifts, you gave each other apps? I'm planning to give keepy.me to my brother and sister-in-love this year. Keepy is a free app (but I'm getting them an upgraded version) that helps parents "keep" kids' memories, such as artwork, schoolwork, milestones, and more, in one place. It helps you stay organized, save your kids' memories, and declutter your home. I love it—and I'm not adding to anyone's clutter (in this case, I'm reducing it).

Kathi's Quick Tips

Again, I asked some of my *brilliant* readers what their best gift-giving ideas were. Here's what a few of them said:

> "My favorite two budget words? Photo calendar. Not the expensive printed kind, but the 'slide your own photos in the slot' kind. It's the perfect handmade gift, both for the craft-challenged and the relative who has everything. I order the calendars and select and print the photos while I wait for the calendars to arrive. The calendars even fit inside the USPS one-price envelopes to make shipping easy. Our family loves them! It's been a great way for us to stay connected with our loved ones scattered all over the country."—Robin

"I was looking for an American Girl doll and posted on Facebook. A friend messaged me that her daughter wanted to sell hers. She's making money and we got a sweet deal! My daughter will not care that it's a used one."—Chantel

"Now that we have three kids and I'm staying home, we work hard to be frugal at holidays. So three years ago, my husband gave his parents the gift of rebuilding their front stairway and doing wiring at their house. I gave a family friend a Shellac-ing of her nails (I retired from my nail salon, and she'd been a client as well as a friend). We've given housecleaning to my mom, who works full-time and is also finishing her master's. We've also cut significantly who we give gifts to during Christmas. I had some friends whose kids I always bought for and who always bought for my kids, and one year, we just laid it out there, 'How'd you like it if instead of buying gifts, we just exchange cookies?' And we were all relieved! I think sometimes it takes just being willing to be the one to bring it up, and there's a lot of relief."—Shannon

"A couple of my girls are on Pinterest. I went to their boards to see if they had anything that I could make. We are making a bunch of things from just scrap wood and sheet metal around the house. I'm more excited about the handmade projects than I am about anything I have bought so far."—Cheryl

The Cookie Dough Exchange

The reasons we now do a Cookie Dough Exchange (CDE) instead of a regular cookie swap are pretty obvious. Who could eat all those cookies at one time? (OK, don't answer that.)

I would go to a traditional cookie exchange and come home with 144 cookies. After my kids picked through and grabbed all their favorites, we were left with a sad collection of broken cookies that strangely all seemed to taste the same after a couple of days. Nice.

With the CDE, there are some clear advantages:

* *Fresh-baked cookies.* You bake only as many as you can eat (or should eat) so you get that fresh-baked-from-the-oven taste instead of sitting-on-a-cheap-paper-plate-for-days taste.

* *Great recipes.* With a dough exchange, you have to include the recipe so people can finish the process. If you discover a dough that you love, you can repeat the process.

* *Spread the joy.* There is no cookie glut. You can pop in a cookie a day, save some for after the New Year, or bake a bunch on the day you have company.

Here are the principles of how a Cookie Dough Exchange works.

1. Figure out the number of participants. If you have twelve people including yourself, you will want to do eleven packets of dough plus one to bake and take (see step 7). If you have only four or five people, perhaps you will all want to double up and bring two

packets of dough per person. Each packet should be portioned out to make approximately twelve cookies.

2. After mixing your dough at home, get it to the ready-to-be-baked stage. That may be little round balls or you could do cookie logs that are ready to be sliced.

3. Whatever shape your cookie dough is in, I suggest that you flash freeze it on a cookie sheet before packaging it. It will make it easier to handle and keep its shape better.

4. I package my dough in large Ziploc bags. Put the dough in the bag and write the baking instructions on the bag. I like to experiment with the cookies and find out what the baking time and temperature is for frozen dough as well as thawed dough.

5. I suggest you avoid doing any cookie that requires a unique shape, like sugar cookies or gingerbread cookies. They will not hold their shape well and will be a pain to package.

6. Print out copies of the recipe to hand out to all the exchangers.

7. Don't forget your extra dozen cookies to bake and take the day of the exchange (purely for sampling purposes, of course).

What's Your Budget?

I want you to avoid the Christmas hangover.

No. I'm not talking about monitoring your intake of eggnog (which, by the way, is not a bad idea). I want you to avoid the financial hangover so many of us have in January.

At no other time of year does the mentality of "eat now, diet later" or "buy now, pay later" dominate more than during the month of December. It's like we're all a bunch of first graders whose teacher left the classroom and we're gonna party.

***

At no other time of year does the mentality of "buy now, pay later" dominate more than during the month of December.

We need to budget our time and money in a way that says, "Here's how I'm being intentional about what I spend and what I spend it on." If we're making a magical Christmas with late nights and overdrawn accounts, the magic only lasts so long.

✳ **Project 7**: What's Your Budget? ✳

Here is what you will need:

✳ A budgeting sheet (you can download a sample at ChristmasProject.org)

Yes, it's a big holiday, and for most of us, it makes up a huge part of our fall and winter expenses. So I want you to spend a little time budgeting what you are going to spend. Here are some areas that you may want to consider:

food	decorations	shipping
gifts	clothes	
donations	cards	

Have a discussion with your husband or whomever you share the money with. I'm not telling you what to budget; I just don't want you to be surprised at the end of the month.

Make It a Clutter-Free Christmas

Got some budget clutter? Here are some things to think about:

✳ Eliminate some categories altogether. How about this year instead of shipping gifts, you just send gift cards to your out-of-town relatives? Or maybe skip the Christmas cards this year and save some serious cash.

✳ Do you really need new clothes for the holidays? Do you have a great outfit from two winters ago that you've buried in the back of the closet? How about some friends you might be able to trade hand-me-downs with for your kids' clothes? Get creative and see if that can be a zero budget item for you.

* If you host the family dinner every year, realize that every dish you ask someone else to bring could be saving you between ten to twenty dollars. This also makes people feel more a part of the celebration instead of invited guests.

Kathi's Quick Tips

I asked some of my readers for their best budgeting tips. Here is the genius that they shared. May it spark some creative ways for you to do what is important to you and yours without completely blowing your budget.

> "I watch the Groupons and see if anything pops up that I can use. Just bought a $20 coupon for $10. This will buy me a couple things when I see a good sale in the next few weeks."—Chantel

> "I look for sales on the items I want to buy, but even more than that, I like to set aside $50 to $100 a month from the beginning of the year so that I have a big chunk of money to spend just on Christmas. Some banks even have Christmas savings accounts."—Rachelle

> "Pay cash whenever possible. It is much easier to lose track of your spending and go over budget when using a debit or credit card. By using cash, it's also easier to keep your gift to your spouse a secret if you have a joint account."—Melody

> "My best advice this time of year is *be patient*. All of those sale signs are enticing, but stores generally offer only a few great deals in an attempt to get you in the door. Don't be tricked into shopping around if you've come just for a deal. Otherwise, you're sure to pay a

higher price than you should have on those extras in your cart. Shopping only for the deals takes some time and planning, so start early. Watch for those 'get you in the door' deals, cash in on those, and leave."—Natasha

"My siblings and I chose to make donations to World Vision or other worthy organizations instead of sending gifts to each other. We enjoy this giving and saving ourselves from the shopping, wrapping, and mailing at Christmas. We set a certain amount we will spend for each of our children and their spouses. Things will change when they add grandchildren to the equation."—Sharon

"We don't exchange gifts with our immediate family. Our kids get plenty spoiled by grandparents, and Grandma and Grandpa are thrilled to be the ones to make their dreams come true. Santa brings one larger gift for the whole family and stuffs our stockings (mostly with shampoo and toothbrushes that I would have to buy for them anyway). Our focus instead is on spending time together."—Renee

"For my thirteen-year-old daughter's teachers and friends, we are making gourmet cupcakes. We are putting them in cute boxes that I bought for a dollar each. It gives us time together and yummy treats for her friends. It also cuts costs. We love cupcake wars, and it is very trendy right now too."—Christie

"A few years back we discovered the Advent Conspiracy (www.adventconspiracy.org). They challenge gift givers to focus on what Christ gave us for Christmas: himself! Instead of buying all kinds of stuff, we now focus on giving our children experiences for us to do together. The other part of the challenge is to take some of the money we would have spent on gifts and give to causes that make a difference in people's lives. Over the last three years, we have given to clean water projects in Guatemala, an orphanage that rescues girls from prostitution in India, and an orphanage in Brazil. Suddenly, that gadget I thought I had to have pales in comparison to these children's basic needs."—Robin

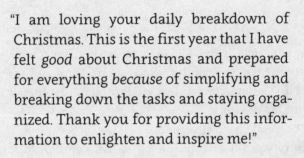

"I am loving your daily breakdown of Christmas. This is the first year that I have felt *good* about Christmas and prepared for everything *because* of simplifying and breaking down the tasks and staying organized. Thank you for providing this information to enlighten and inspire me!"

Jen

Catch-Up Day (and a Bonus Project)

Today is a catch-up day. Use today to catch up on anything you feel you're running behind on. And for extra credit, if you're married, I have a Bonus Project that will help you and your spouse get into the holiday spirit.

Roger and I have a tradition.

Every year, we each pick a few special items for each other (lotions, super-fancy chocolates, a silky robe, silly boxers) and wrap them in red paper and put them under the tree. Nobody else is allowed to be around when the red gifts are unwrapped, and I can say with confidence that our red gifts are hands down our favorite gifts every year. Hands down.

I love this tradition, and love finding something that will make Roger smile and know he is loved. But as we had our special gift exchange last year, I got to thinking: *Why do I save all of my red gifts for Christmas morning when the truth is, I need to pour into my man often? Like every day?*

> ***
> I love finding something that will make
> Roger smile and know he is loved.

So this year, I'm starting a new tradition. I will, of course, be wrapping a couple of red gifts and putting them under the tree, but I'm also going to do something a little extra once a week in December for Roger to help him know he is loved this Christmas. Nothing big, just a little something to show him that even though I am crazy busy and the to-do list is a mile long, I still love him first and most.

And for today's bonus project, I'm asking you to do the same.

✳ **Bonus Project**: Help Your Spouse Get into the Holiday Spirit ✳

Today, I want you to think of one thing you can do for your husband or wife to make the season special. Try to think of some small (or if you want, big!) way you can bless your spouse and show them they are your priority, even though the season is getting hectic.

Here are some ideas to get you started as you plan:

✳ Head to the bakery and buy a Christmas cookie or brownie. Slip it to your spouse and let them know they don't have to share.

✳ Treat your spouse to a relaxing massage. (You can do it yourself or book an appointment at the spa.)

✳ Send your husband or wife a text message and let them know that you've reserved the night just for them. Wink, wink. Nudge, nudge.

✳ Take care of a chore that your spouse normally does.

✳ Make hot cocoa and share it by the fire while you talk.

✳ Rent a Christmas movie and watch it together.

* Whip up your spouse's favorite dinner or pick up a favorite food for takeout.

* Offer to shop for your spouse's boss or great-aunt. Do it happily without complaining.

* Offer to give your spouse an hour of peace and quiet.

* Write an encouraging note to your husband or wife. Leave it on the bathroom mirror.

* Plan a date night.

PROJECT 9

Gifts for Out-of-Town Friends and Family

My life was so simple. Then I married Roger.

You see, my whole family lives within a two-hour drive of my home. We get together for holidays and exchange gifts like the Norman Rockwell painting says we're supposed to do. Then I had to marry a Southern boy.

When Roger was looking for his first grown-up job as a senior at Purdue University, he told God his requirements. "God, I will go anywhere except California." Yeah, that's a good idea. Tell God what you won't do.

So twenty-five years ago, Roger got a job in Cupertino with HP, and he has been a California boy ever since. The only problem is that his whole family lives in Georgia and they all celebrate Christmas. And somehow, when we were first married, I forgot that their gifts required an extra step or two.

So today, your project is to get your plan together for any out-of-town gifts. There are three approaches you can take:

1. Order all your gifts online and have them shipped from the company.

2. Buy gifts and ship them out from home.

3. Make sure you've married a local boy or stop talking to out-of-state relatives and friends.

✳ **Project 9:** Gifts for Out-of-Town Friends and Family ✳

I'm not expecting you to buy and ship all your out-of-town gifts today, but I do want you to think specifically about what you are going to get for whom and by what day you need to have it in the mail.

✳✳✳

Think about what you are going to get for whom and by what day you need to have it in the mail.

Make It a Clutter-Free Christmas

✳ Think e-gifts for any of your out-of-town relatives and friends. They are easy to send, don't clutter up someone's home, and you don't have to worry about wrapping.

✳ Is there a gift that's easy to mail that everyone would like? Roger's mom sends us and others a selection of nuts from Georgia every year. Keep it simple.

Kathi's Quick Tips: Mailable Gifts

My definition of mailable gifts is anything that can be mailed in a bubble envelope or one of the post office's Priority Mail envelopes and get there in the same condition it was mailed in. Here are some ideas of things that are easy to mail.

Rubber stamp kit (for kids). All it takes is a rubber stamp or two, an inkpad, and some paper.

T-shirt. Recently my friend Erin told her kids that I was having a bad day (my husband's stepmom had just passed away suddenly) and asked them what they could send me to cheer me up. Joey, her oldest, said, "A UT shirt, of course." Joey naturally assumed that someone he loves would be rooting for the University of Texas. Even though I don't live in Texas. Or like football. But because it's from Joey, it's my favorite T-shirt ever.

Table runner. I usually shy away from buying things to decorate someone else's house, but a table runner is a small commitment (not something that has to be out every day), and it's easy to mail. I love Pier 1 or Cost Plus to find funky ones. A good holiday one is great since it's brought out for only a few days a year.

Sharpie markers and fun office supplies. I am an office supply junkie. I think it calls me back to my youth and those first days of September when I spent hours organizing and reorganizing my school supplies because I was convinced that if I had a perfectly organized binder, it would lead to the Best. Year. Ever.

Seeds or bulbs. How could you better send hope for spring than seeds or bulbs in the mail? It makes my wannabe green thumb itch just thinking about it.

Goat from World Vision. One Christmas my kids got me a sponsorship for a goat for a family in Africa. To represent the goat, my daughters found instructions online on how to fold a towel into the shape of a goat (like the towel animals on cruise ships). If you want to put something in the mail to represent your sponsorship, here are some step-by-step instructions to fold your own goat, origami-style: www.origami-instructions.com/origami-goat-face.html.

Museum pass. What a great gift to give to an entire family.

Vanilla beans. Every year I make big batches of vanilla extract by slicing the beans the long way and letting them soak in vodka or rum for at least six weeks. For faraway friends, I will send them bottles of vanilla. But for my Pinterest-type friends (the DIY crowd), I just send some exotic beans through the mail and let them make their own trip to the liquor store. Trust me, your foodie friend will be thrilled.

Ebooks. As an author, I thank you in advance.

Audiobooks. My favorite gift to give—and receive.

Magazine subscription. I know people especially appreciate a subscription renewal for their favorite periodical.

Kitchen accessories. Pot holders, towels, tablecloths, napkins, and cutting boards are flat, easily mailable, and seem to always need replacing.

Nationality box. One year a friend who knew me when I lived in Japan went to a Japanese market and loaded up on popular candies, origami paper, Pocky (a type of cookie dipped in chocolate), cute tissue packs, chopsticks, and stickers. Everything was in pinks and light green, and it was the prettiest package I ever opened.

Other ideas. Here's a random bunch of other ideas to help spark your creativity: superhero cape, bow tie, coffee and tea, nuts, socks, fashion tape, mittens, fabric bags, coasters, cookbooks, decks of cards, girl stuff such as hairbands, jewelry, and nail appliqués.

Gather Your Elf Supplies

Can you believe that you are ten days in? I hope you're getting to really, truly enjoy your season. I hope you:

* feel ahead for this year
* feel ahead for next year
* know what you're going to get each person on your list
* have a feeling of accomplishment

*Project 10: Gather Your Elf Supplies *

Originally this project was going to be "Buy Your Stuff," but I know that all of us probably have enough gift wrap, tags, and ribbon to supply Santa's workshop. Problem is, most of us find it December 26.

So dig through your basement, garage, spare closet, or under the bed and gather together:

* wrapping paper
* ribbon
* tissue paper
* tags

* scotch tape
* scissors
* gift bags and boxes

Get all this stuff in one place so that when you have to go into elf mode, you're not running all over the house. This would also be the time to purchase anything that you are short on. I end up buying tape every single year.

***

Get all this stuff in one place so that when you have to go into elf mode, you're not running all over the house.

Now, where are you going to keep all those supplies during this season?

Make It a Clutter-Free Christmas

I would love for you to have an "away space" so your wrapping supplies are not on the living room table for the entire month of December. Is there a place in your coat closet, a drawer in your dining room, or a shelf in your utility closet that is still within reach, but isn't in the middle of all the action in your house? That would be the perfect place to stash your stuff.

For all the little things that I need to keep together (scissors, tape, tags), I use a cleaning caddy with a handle that can be easily moved. Having everything together makes wrapping easy and keeps me from putting it off.

Kathi's Quick Tips

Here are some other wrapping hints:

Use it up. Instead of opening a brand-new roll of paper, use up all the leftover rolls you have. That way there is less to store.

Use what you have. If you have some small branches left over from the tree you pruned, why not tie some small twigs onto your gifts. Have some small ornaments that you aren't going to use on your tree? Tie them onto a gift, or write on them with a Sharpie to make a festive gift tag.

Make photo tags. Have a photo of Fido you just adore? Make copies and tie them onto your gifts as a fun gift tag everyone will adore.

Use fabric, ribbons, and buttons. These are a few of my favorite things—to decorate packages with. Use up your leftovers from that craft project that just didn't turn out right. Raid the jar of buttons you've been keeping in your laundry room.

Use game pieces. Spell out the recipient's name with Scrabble letters attached with double-sided tape, use playing cards as gift tags, or create permanent gift tags with poker chips and Sharpie markers.

Wrap a map. Use an old map to wrap a gift for the travel enthusiast in your life.

Get Your Recipes Together

Each of our kids has a favorite food they *confirm in advance* will be prepared by me or my hubby each Christmas. Here's a portion of what's on our must-have list. I've included the recipes for several of these at the back of the book:

* cranberry no-bake cheesecake
* pumpkin no-bake cheesecake
* artichoke dip
* bruschetta
* broccoli casserole
* ratatouille
* drunken turkey (turkey brined in white wine and spices)

In years past I've spent a lot of time and energy going through various cookbooks, computer searches, and junk drawer layers looking for all these recipes—but no more! This year they were all sitting in the Christmas Binder just where they were supposed to be.

Project 11: Get Your Recipes Together

You have a tab in your Christmas Binder for your family's favorite recipes. Now is the time to fill up that tab with the traditional recipes your family loves.

The other wonderful thing about having all your recipes

together is that when your kids decide they want to bring your family recipes to their in-laws' homes, you can copy everything at once.

Here is what you will need:

* Page protectors
* Your favorite recipes

The process is pretty simple, really. Here's what works well for me:

1. Insert the page protectors into your Christmas Binder.

2. Gather into one place all the cookbooks, recipe cards, magazine pages, and so on that hold your favorite holiday recipes.

3. Use your scanner to copy your favorite recipes onto 8½ x 11 pages. If you don't own a scanner, you'll need to visit your local copy center for this step.

4. Print any recipes you have stored on your computer onto 8½ x 11 pages.

5. While watching TV, load all your recipes into page protectors.

6. If you have some extra binder tabs, go ahead and sort the recipes into main categories:

   * Appetizers
   * Salads
   * Side Dishes
   * Main Dishes
   * Desserts
   * Cookies (Yes, cookies get their own category.)

Make It a Clutter-Free Christmas

No one gets the prize for collecting the most recipes they will never use. Trim your binder down to only the recipes you use and love.

***

Trim your binder down to only the
recipes you use and love.

If you have several cookbooks that contain only one or two recipes that you use, copy the pages and get rid of the books. Give them to a friend so they can discover their favorite recipes! By the way, it is perfectly legal to copy recipes out of a book that you own for your personal use within your home. (Because I know some of you were wondering.)

Kathi's Quick Tips

I love having all my recipes on 8½ x 11 pages in the binder, each in its own page protector. When I pull out a recipe to use it, I leave it in the page protector so that it has its own personal splashguard.

I promise you will thank me for this project when it comes time to get your food shopping list together.

Catch Up on Your Project

Today is your day to just catch up on everything. We're just beyond the halfway point of the 21 days and really, all I want you to do today is stop, catch your breath, see where you are, and figure out what area you need to spend some additional time in.

Easy, right?

"I am usually well-organized, so many of these projects are easily being checked off the list. But I am totally loving and appreciating your advice on making out a big calendar page and posting all the doings on the fridge. This is enabling my entire family to prepare for what is coming and to be a part of helping out. The calendar making is somehow relieving to me, shifting the Christmas actions to becoming a family responsibility and not just mine."

Beth

Decor Day

There are multiple reasons why our family members are not collectors of delicate things.

My mom started a collection for my daughter, Kimberly, of figurines called Snowbabies. These statuettes depict small children in snowsuits sledding, skiing, and generally frolicking in the snow. They are made in unglazed porcelain. While I'm not a fan of tiny figurines (I may have been traumatized by the "no-touch" policy of the Hummels of my youth), these are actually pretty cute.

Every year, not only would Kimberly look forward to receiving a new one, but her collection of Snowbabies was the first thing she went to unpack as we started to decorate for Christmas.

Lacking a mantel in our home, I hung all of our stockings on a shelf in the playroom of our tiny house. After hanging the stockings, I covered the shelf in snow-like fluff and nestled the six Snowbabies among the snow to create our own little winter wonderland.

Until later that day when I heard the *crash*.

My son, Justen, just hoping that Santa had come a little early to fill the stockings with Gummi Bears, decided to tug his stocking down to see what was inside. Along with the stocking, Justen pulled down the entire shelf, and all those Babies came crashing to the floor.

> * * *
> Let's just say that figurine restoration
> is not one of my giftings.

To this day, we still display those Snowbabies, but now they are more customized for our family. Let's just say that figurine restoration is not one of my giftings. Those Snowbabies have some bumps and bruises, but they are survivors. That makes us love them a little bit more.

I have to admit that Roger does the majority of the decorating around our house. (There's a reason he's a lighting designer. He likes bright shiny things.)

* **Project 13:** Get Some of Your Decorating Done *

Here is what you will need:

* * Your Christmas decor boxes from last year
* * A Christmas tree removal bag (You can purchase these at any hardware store or general store, like Target. These bags keep you from getting pine needles all over your floor when you take the tree down and drag it to the curb. The trick—remembering to put it around the base of the tree when you first put the tree up!)
* * Ornament hooks

Here are some of the things you may want to consider working on:

* * Get and decorate your tree.

* Put away some of your everyday stuff so you'll have room for your Christmas decor.

* Swap out your regular dishes for your Christmas dishes.

* Decorate outside.

Make It a Clutter-Free Christmas

Let It Go

One of the other big helps for Christmas decor is to get rid of anything that you are no longer decorating with—those pink snowmen you bought during your *Miami Vice* Christmas phase, or that stack of Christmas cards from people you no longer connect with (and maybe don't really like). The less you have to sort through, the easier the decorating process will be.

Treasure or Trash

If you have broken ornaments, today would be a great day to get out the superglue and repair them. If they aren't worthy of the time that it will take to fix them? Pitch 'em.

Repurpose for Christmas

You don't need to redecorate your entire house for the holidays. I have some awesome wood-and-glass bird cages that are in my living room all year long. Instead of taking them down for Christmas, I fill them up with some inexpensive Christmas bulbs. I love them so much that I kept them up through February this year.

Kathi's Quick Tips

* Every year I take a plain door in our house (this year it's the door to our furnace) and wrap it like a big present. Then as Christmas cards come into the house, I

tape them directly to the door. The envelopes I save
in a Ziploc in my Christmas Binder to check for new
addresses.

* As I'm unpacking holiday decorations, I do two
  things:

  1. I pull out anything I'm not planning to decorate
  with and set it aside for charity. I would much
  rather my Christmas decor end up at a charity shop
  in November or December than in January when
  I'm packing it all away.

  2. As I pull out the decor, I use those empty
  containers that have held all my decorations to
  hold some of the home decor I have out the other
  ten months of the year.

* Get the rest of your decor in the holiday mood. I have
  three fat ceramic chickens that Roger bought me on
  our first anniversary. I love those chickens too much
  to put them away at Christmas, so I just give each of
  them a red bow for the holidays, and they fit right in.

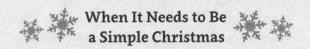

When It Needs to Be a Simple Christmas

There could be a million reasons why you are time crunched this Christmas—family obligation, a huge project at work. Here's one question I would ask you to consider: Do you feel a time crunch every Christmas? If so, I strongly recommend that you not only make some accommodations this year, but take a hard look at your own expectations for the holiday season.

Sometimes we are so afraid of making changes because we're sure that everyone is going to be so disappointed by what we're not doing. The reality probably is that we're doing a lot of things that are important only to us, and possibly only for tradition's sake.

Here is what I've learned about time and Christmas:

1. *You need to ask your family what is important.* Immediately stop doing anything that your family doesn't find important to their own holiday celebration.

2. *You are the one putting the most pressure on you.* Most of us have some picture of what Christmas should look like, but I'm guessing that much of what that picture contains could be done away with when times are hard. Do you need a full-blown Christmas tree or would a tiny one that sits on your mantel do? Do you need to have the turkey with all the trimmings or would a Christmas dinner of Chinese takeout be OK for a year when you aren't up to cooking?

3. *Everyone gets a pass.* Give yourself a pass—and the rest of the people in your life a pass as well. Have the conversation. Because both my husband and I had surgeries within a month of Christmas one year, I told

my extended family that we were happy to host, but I would not be buying or cooking the entire meal. My mom wasn't in a position to host, but she was happy to shop and cook for us at my house with the help of all the kids. Everyone contributed, but no one was stretched.

4. *The saying, "It just won't be Christmas without..." must be banned from your vocabulary.* The only thing you need in order to celebrate Christmas is a relationship with your Savior. I'm not trying to get all Pharisee-ish here, but we must remember that everything else is the fudge on the ice cream that is our true reason for celebrating. Don't make yourself crazy with ideas like "It just won't be Christmas if I don't put all the ornaments on the tree," or "It just won't be Christmas if we don't see *The Nutcracker* this year." Yes, it will still be Christmas. It will just be a Christmas where you aren't stretching yourself too thin.

5. *Changing traditions gives you freedom.* So you put up a tree with lights only, no ornaments (like we are doing this year). Think how much fun it's going to be to see those ornaments next year! Tradition can be a merciless slave driver.

Prep Your Kitchen

My kids still tell the story—fifteen years later—of the day we didn't eat Christmas dinner. It's part of our family history. Do I regret my mistake? No. (I'd do almost anything for a good story.) But I've learned from that mistake, and we will never, ever have twelve appetizers again.

I knew I should have made a list. My work schedule had been crazy, and we had loads of family coming over for Christmas Eve. I knew what I wanted to cook for our dinner—a big ham with all the sides: potatoes, both scalloped and mashed, green-bean casserole, salad, stuffing, rolls (can you tell we love our carbs), cranberry sauce, and asparagus. Yes, it was going to be an amazing meal.

> ***
>
> I knew I should have made a list.

I was handling the ham and all the sides. So when my mom asked what she could bring, I told her, "Could you bring some appetizers?" She said no problem. A few weeks later, as we got closer to our celebration, my brother asked what he could bring. Knowing that I had the main meal covered, I said, "How about a few hors d'oeuvres?"

And then my in-laws asked what they could bring. Knowing that dinner would take a while, I asked them to bring a few snacks to help tide us over until the meal would be ready. And in case anyone was late, I prepared a few cheese-and-cracker plates and made some artichoke dip.

The day of the meal, after we all gathered together and spent the next several hours grazing through all the pre-food, no one ate a bite of dinner. Not. One. Bite.

Now there may be a day in the future where we decide to have an all-appetizer Christmas meal. (In fact, that sounds like an amazing idea. The wheels in my head are turning...) But a little planning and a list on the fridge would have saved us from a lot of waste—and me being the central character in "The Christmas Dinner that Never Got Eaten."

A little planning up front can save you from such disasters.

✳ **Project 14:** Prep Your Kitchen ✳

So today's project is to spend a little more time in the kitchen. Here are some things that you might want to get ahead on:

* ✳ Create your meal plan for the rest of the month.

* ✳ Plan out your Christmas dinner and your shopping list.

* ✳ Shop for your nonperishables.

* ✳ Make the list of what you need to buy at the last minute so it's fresh.

* ✳ Pull out your serving platters, roasting pans, cake stands, or anything else that you'll need.

* ✳ Pull together your baking list.

Make It a Clutter-Free Christmas

Clear all the clutter from your kitchen. Pack away absolutely anything you can to clear as much counter space as possible. Go through your pantry and throw out any food that's past its "best by" date and taking up space, and generally get a fresh start in the busiest room of the house this time of year.

* * *

Pack away absolutely anything you can to clear as much counter space as possible.

Kathi's Quick Tips

Not only are we a blended family, but we are starting to add some new family members. Shaun and Amanda have been together for a couple of years and are now in the midst of wedding plans. So not only do our kids have another parent to split the holiday with, we are also dealing with significant other's families and making it work.

Our new plan these past few years has been to have one big traditional meal each year, and then we do something fun and different for the other holidays.

For instance, this year we will have everyone at our house for Thanksgiving (including some friends and our new neighbors from China), and we'll make the turkey, ham, potatoes, stuffing, rolls, salad, and pies. Lots of pies.

But for our Christmas celebration, we are going much simpler. This year? Pizza fondue. In years past? We've barbecued, made a big pot of chili and homemade bread, raviolis, and tamales. Sometimes the best thing you can do is pick a theme and go with it. Maybe it's a crab boil or lasagna. But keeping it simple and different from your other holidays is the idea.

So when it's time to do the traditional dinner, I ask each family member this one simple question: What is the one dish that you *must* have for Christmas?

That way, we can make sure that everyone has their favorites.

> * * *
>
> I ask each family member this one simple question: What is the one dish that you *must* have for Christmas?

I keep all our traditional family favorites in my Christmas Binder, and if I see anything interesting that I'd like to try, I'll print it off and throw it in the binder. That way, when I sit down to plan, I have everything in one place, and I don't have to waste time or paper reprinting recipes.

Here are some of the things I like to do in advance if I will be hosting our huge Christmas dinner (or a lot of little celebrations along the way):

* Make a calendar of all the events we'll be hosting, along with any event that we'll be attending that we are bringing food to. This helps me wrap my head around all the extras we'll be doing this season, and it helps me estimate the amount we'll need to put aside budget-wise for the next several weeks.

* If I'm going to be attending a lot of parties, I try to sign up to bring the same dish to each one. It's far

easier to bring our famous artichoke dip to four different parties than to come up with four different dishes
(and so far, no one has ever turned down our artichoke dip).

* After you make a list of everything you will need
  throughout the season, go through your cupboards
  and pantry and see what you already have instead of
  buying everything on your list. You may have all the
  canned pumpkin you need left over from your fall
  baking kick. Also, note if you need to stock up on
  resealable plastic bags.

Get Those Stockings Ready

I come from a family who raced downstairs at the crack of dawn to flip our stockings upside down and rifle through our big pile of loot. It was just the way it was done. So naturally, on our first Christmas together, I ran—I mean, walked quickly—down the stairs and dumped my stocking to find…nothing.

Turns out Roger's ex-wife had been the keeper of the stockings at his house.

It really didn't bother me (I promise), but I think Roger felt bad. So the next year, he informed me that he had bought something for my stocking. And I raced—I mean, walked like an adult—down the stairs to dump my stocking to find…twelve bottles of hand sanitizer. Twelve bottles.

Again, I wasn't offended (after all, hand sanitizer has its place), but I did make a promise to myself: Every year, I was going to buy myself something special for my own stocking—nothing big or extravagant but maybe a lotion I've been wanting or a pair of earrings. A little Christmas treat for myself.

And I have to admit, I am pretty good at playing Santa.

✳ **Project 15:** Get Those Stockings Ready ✳

Today's project is to get ready for stockings at your house. (Don't worry, you don't have to do all the shopping today, but you do have to get ready for it.) Here's what I want you to do:

Come Up with a Plan

It's really easy to go overboard (or underboard) with stockings. So my first suggestion is to come up with a plan on what you want to buy and how much you want to spend. For example, maybe your plan is to spend twenty-five dollars on each stocking and get eight items for each person.

Come Up with a System

In my gift closet, I keep a resealable bag for each person with their name on it. As I gather up little treats for each person, I wrap them and keep them in the appropriate bag. When it comes time to fill the individual stockings, all I do is dump the contents of each bag into the appropriate stocking.

Shop Slowly but Surely

Going shopping for stocking stuffers all at once can be daunting. I make it a point to pick up little things I see throughout the year and slip them into those handy resealable bags. That said, if you haven't already started, make it your goal to pick up one or two things for stockings each time you go shopping from now until Christmas, and you will slowly whittle away at your list.

* * *

Make it your goal to pick up one or two things for stockings each time you go shopping, and you will slowly whittle away at your list.

Make It a Clutter-Free Christmas

For years I bought little toys and treats just so the stockings would be full. But there's a reason those things at the entrance to Target are only a dollar—that's about how much you will use the item (a dollar's worth) before it becomes a piece of clutter in your room, or more likely, your kid's room. When thinking about stocking stuffers, buy things that are small and will be loved and used. Keep it practical, useful, and fun.

Kathi's Quick Tips

On this project, instead of giving you quick tips, I'm going to list twenty-five fun, inexpensive, and creative stocking stuffer ideas. Enjoy.

1. Chocolate gold coins
2. Toothbrushes
3. Dental floss
4. Fun flavors of K-Cup coffee pods
5. Hair things (like rubber bands or barrettes)
6. Playing cards
7. Thank-you notes (These are supposed to inspire the kids to actually write the notes...it happens about 50 percent of the time.)
8. Starbucks gift cards
9. Little jars of syrup, jam, or jelly
10. Small tools (What guy doesn't want a cute little screwdriver to carry around in his car?)
11. iTunes gift cards with song suggestions to download
12. Lip balm (I love EOS Smooth Sphere lip balms.)
13. Nice pens
14. Gum or mints

15. Hand sanitizer (Perhaps not twelve bottles though.)

16. Fun spices or spice mixes

17. Amazon gift cards for books

18. Movie tickets

19. Travel containers of shampoo, body wash, or conditioner

20. Coupon for a back rub or help with a project

21. A journal

22. A favorite candy from the person's childhood

23. Trading cards (baseball or football or Pokémon)

24. A specialty chocolate bar (Bonus points if you find a flavor like maple bacon or chili lime.)

25. An orange (It smells wonderful and fits nicely in the toe of a stocking.)

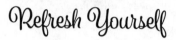

Refresh Yourself

Whew. You've been working hard, haven't you?

The Christmas season is always a frantic array of hustle and bustle. It's enough to sometimes make you want to scream. Literally.

I remember a day last year when I had a teensy bit too much on my to-do list. And by that, I mean I had attempted to not only go shopping for gifts for fourteen people, but I also thought it might be a good idea to go grocery shopping for nonperishables, buy my wrapping paper, go to the post office, and stop by the church office to deliver muffins. All on the same day. Oh, and I also had to work.

I realized at about 4:00 p.m. that I had attempted too much when I snapped at Roger for no apparent reason. And Roger— bless his heart—just sat me down and said that we needed a *How I Met Your Mother* marathon night. So we snuggled on the couch, ate takeout, and watched TV for about thirteen billion hours. And the next morning, guess what happened? Good Kathi came back.

And I was able to make it through my entire to-do list without a single meltdown.

***
We all need a break this time of year.

We all need a break this time of year. So today, before you get to that point of no return, your project is to do something really fun just for yourself.

✳ **Project 16:** Get Some You Time ✳

I know it's hard to find time for you, especially during the holidays. I also know that you may be tempted to skip this project because women are notoriously unselfish and are often willing to sacrifice whatever time or money that could be for themselves for their family. But I'm not letting you out of this. You need this. And you will be a better mom, wife, and friend this holiday season if you take some time for yourself.

So your job today is to find one way to refresh yourself. I've listed some ideas below to get you started, but use your imagination and do something that you know will help you wake up tomorrow feeling ready to face the day. And to face Project 17.

Refresh Yourself Ideas

* ✳ Take a bubble bath.
* ✳ Spend an hour reading a great novel by the fire. Make sure to make yourself a decadent cup of coffee to enjoy while you're reading.
* ✳ Go on a long walk in the park. Even better if you can invite a friend to go with you.
* ✳ Grab lunch or coffee with a friend.
* ✳ Grab lunch or coffee by yourself and revel in the silence.
* ✳ Pick up a cupcake or a brownie and enjoy every single bite.
* ✳ Mindlessly browse Facebook for an hour.
* ✳ Mindlessly browse Pinterest for an hour. Don't allow yourself to repin or plan on making a single thing.

* Get a makeover at the mall.

* Call a friend and talk for as long as you can about whatever you want.

* Go on a date night with your man.

* Take a Pilates class at the gym. Spend an inordinate amount of time in the steam room afterward.

* Watch a Christmas movie.

* Make a Christmas playlist and blast it through your speakers all day long.

* Sit in front of the Christmas tree and just think and pray.

"Oh, lady, am I loving this project. I had an old Christmas binder from a different organizing website that for me never worked. *This* is all practical, doable stuff that I've (mostly) been able to keep up with! Your stocking tip to assign each family member a Ziploc bag and use it to keep all their stocking items in until Christmas Eve is *genius*! So simple...really a duh moment for me. I love the binder. I'm a sucker for office supplies and making things look organized, and now having a copy of my Christmas recipes all in one place."

Tonya

Ship Those Boxes Out

I'm not one to cry in public, but the post office at Christmastime is enough to make a grown woman weep. And then binge eat candy canes. And I do know this from experience.

A few years ago, before I discovered the magic of USPS.com (more on that later), I made the entirely unwise choice to brave the post office on December 16 while I was (a) hungry and (b) tired.

✳✳✳

A few years ago, I made the entirely unwise choice to brave the post office on December 16 while I was (a) hungry and (b) tired.

It didn't look very bad when I walked in. Just twenty odd people in line, a few boxes lining the edges of the building. But as I stood there watching the line creep to the front with record-breaking slowness, I realized that I had been mistaken. Because not only did each person in front of me have at least 243 packages to ship, but each of them was also cranky, tired, and as ready to get out of there as I was.

Oh, and they were happy to tell the postal workers about their angst when they finally got to the front of the line, adding a good five minutes to each person's already excruciatingly long turn.

There is a better way, ladies. And today, I'm going to tell you about it so you can get all of those packages shipped out and to your loved ones in plenty of time for them to *ooh* and *aah* at them under the tree.

And just think of how great you'll feel to get through shipping day without eating a single candy cane.

✳ **Project 17**: Ship Your Boxes ✳

Get all of your packages shipped out today, and if you forgot someone, don't worry. Tomorrow is online shopping day so you can finish up then.

Make It a Clutter-Free Christmas

I have two tips that I think will make today's project one of your easiest ones:

1. Learn how to ship using USPS.com (they have a whole shipping guide if you've never done it before).

2. Use Priority Mail boxes.

Why do I love those Priority Mail boxes so?

✳ You can schedule Priority Mail to be picked up at your house the next day.

✳ Boxes with preprinted, prepaid labels from USPS.com can just be dropped off at the post office. You don't need to wait in line.

I like to use the Priority boxes that you don't have to weigh— those prepaid boxes you can just keep stuffing until you can barely close them, and the rate stays the same.

Kathi's Quick Tips

* Wrap a bunch of smaller gifts and then place them in a Priority Mail box to send to one family.

* Remember you can't send anything liquid or fragile, so make sure your gifts meet postal service requirements before you wrap them.

* You can schedule a pickup at your house or, if all your packages are labeled and paid for through USPS.com, you can just drop the whole stack off at the post office. My husband and I make this a two-person operation, especially around the holidays when there's limited parking. I'm the driver, and he hops out with all the packages and puts them on the counter at the post office. I drive back around and pick him up. Quick and easy.

Get Online

I intended to be one of the last holdouts.

I was going to go to the actual stores and handpick my gifts, and I was going to wrap them and box them and label them and then stand in the hours-long line at the post office to ship them for my loved ones.

This was "walking both ways uphill to school in the snow" material, you guys. But I was going to stick with it. And do it well. Because my friends and family needed personally taped and shipped boxes from me, darn it.

But then this little thing called Amazon Prime was released. And my word, I could click a little button, and in two days, the box magically arrived at my loved one's house with a little gift note. For free. And all I had to do was kick back in my desk chair, wearing jammies and drinking coffee, and find something awesome to send.

> ✳✳✳
>
> I'm way less cranky at the end of the
> day when I don't have to stand in line
> at the mall or the post office.

I'll just come out and say it. This has changed me. Amazon Prime has made me a better gift giver. A better shopper. And honestly, a better wife because I'm way less cranky at the end of the day when I don't have to stand in line at the mall or the post office.

For today's project, I'm going to have you finish up your shopping online. Sure, you can still pick up that extra-special something for your husband at that cute little chocolate shop down the road, but for distant family members and such, today is your day to get your shopping done.

✳ **Project 18**: Get Online ✳

Of course, not everyone has Amazon Prime and not every perfect gift is on Amazon, so before you do your online shopping, I want to make sure you know the best places to shop online. So I asked my readers, and they submitted dozens of fantastic "fishing holes" so we can all be faster, cheaper, better this year.

Make It a Clutter-Free Christmas

Here are a few favorite ideas, both mine and from my readers.

* Zulily. Zulily is a flash sale site that has adorable things for kids, women, and the home, all on sale for at least 30 percent off. There is a catch: Zulily is notoriously slow at shipping, but they do have a little gift icon on items they guarantee by Christmas, so I would stick to those.

* Zappos offers free shipping and free returns of clothes, shoes, and household goods.

* Amazon printable gift cards. In case you forgot to get your father-in-law a gift (Who me? Never.), you can pop on there and send him a gift card that will arrive in his inbox on Christmas morning, as if you'd planned it that way all along. You can even email him a list of your favorite book suggestions to go with the gift card.

* If you're buying for a group of people, think of a food treat they could all share. Vermont Brownie Company (www.vermontbrowniecompany.com) makes the best brownies I have ever tasted, and they ship everywhere.

* Got a foodie in your life? Try a locally produced food item to be delivered. Last year for Christmas I sent many of my friends garlic products or Cowgirl Creamery cheeses (www.cowgirlcreamery.com), both local to me here in Silicon Valley. Local and the best cheese I've ever tasted.

Kathi's Quick Tips

* Write a list of who you are shopping for and how much you want to spend for each before you sit down to online shop. It's easy to get carried away when you're online, so it's important to have a game plan.

* Use RetailMeNot (www.retailmenot.com) to search out a coupon code before you check out at each place.

* If a site has a deal like "spend $50, get free shipping," try to buy two presents there. Most places will ship your purchases to different locations.

Take Off Your Apron and Grab Your Pencil

I've been known to nail Christmas dinner.

What can I say? I love to cook and I love to plan. Generally, I plan the meal long in advance, get all the recipes printed and ingredients gathered, and make a pretty amazing meal for my family on the big day.

But the weeks leading up to Christmas? Well, let's just say that Roger has been known to affectionately call them "the cereal days." I cook dinner nearly every night all year long, but prior to Christmas I get sidetracked planning for the big day and forget about all the days leading up to it.

> ✳✳✳
>
> Roger has been known to affectionately call the weeks leading up to Christmas "the cereal days."

And so we eat...well, cereal. And yogurt. And crackers and cheese.

This year, I made a promise to myself that I would not do this. And so I started planning our pre-Christmas meals way ahead. Like before Thanksgiving ahead. It seemed a bit crazy at the time, but here's what I ended up doing as a result of my early planning:

* I chopped up leftover Thanksgiving turkey and separated it into one- and two-cup bags. I froze these and used them to add to turkey noodle soup, casseroles, enchiladas, and more.

* Every time I cooked in early-to-mid December, I made sure to cook a LeftOvers On Purpose (LOOP) meal. That way I was able to freeze some extra meals for those busy days.

* In the days right before Christmas, I planned simple, wholesome meals that would feed us well without costing a ton.

You know what? It was magical. I had dinner—a real dinner—on the table every night, and I still had time to obsess over the chicken crepes recipe my mom makes for the big day. And because this was so helpful to me, your project for today is to do some meal planning—not just for your Christmas dinner but for the days that come before.

* **Project 19:** Spend Some Time in the Kitchen *

Today's project is to spend a little more time in the kitchen—but there is a catch. I don't want you to bake any cookies, to prep any casseroles, or even to make a freezer meal. What I want you to do is plan your meal plan for from now until Christmas. Yes, for that long. Because the next couple of weeks will be crazy busy, but your family will still have to eat.

***

Plan your meal plan for from now
until Christmas. Yes, for that long.

Won't it be nice to have a bunch of easy, healthy meals planned ahead? So today, take off your apron, grab a piece of paper (already three-hole punched to fit in your Christmas Binder), and take the time to:

* Create your meal plan for the rest of the month. Yes, I know it's a lot, but figure out what you're going to have for dinner every night from now until Christmas.

* Plan your baking list so you know what you need to bake and when you're going to do it.

* Plan out your Christmas dinner.

* Write a shopping list for all the meals, your baking, and Christmas dinner. Divide the list into two parts, the nonperishables and the perishables.

* Shop for your nonperishables and the next few days' meals. If you don't have time today, set a time in the near future when you'll do this.

* Make a list of the things you'll need to buy at the last minute so they are fresh.

Make It a Clutter-Free Christmas

Plan on making at least two LOOP meals a week. Cook twice, eat four times.

Use up what you have. We made it a goal to use up any food in our freezer and pantry by the end of the year. Besides, eating from your existing stock is much cheaper and will help with the extra expenses during the holidays.

Kathi's Quick Tips

* Even if your meal plan is grilled cheese or PB and J, write it down. It will feel good to have a plan.

* Pick up some good quality frozen meals (or make your own) so you always have something to pull out of the freezer.

* When in doubt, make a soup. I can almost always make a decent soup out of whatever leftovers I have at home.

* Check out my book *The "What's for Dinner?" Solution* for good recipes for LOOP meals and freezer meals.

* Go easy on yourself for Christmas dinner. Yes, that recipe that has three weeks' worth of steps and 423 ingredients looks delicious, but I'm guessing the much simpler recipe with half the steps and a quarter of the ingredients will also be good.

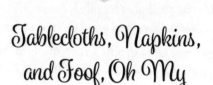

Tablecloths, Napkins, and Foof, Oh My

I'm still notorious for what I affectionately call "Thomas the Tank Engine Christmas."

It was the pre-Pinterest era, which meant that we had to get all our holiday ideas from magazines and books. But I had done it. After scouring *Good Housekeeping* and *Sunset*, I had come up with a plan for a beautiful holiday table. I bought a centerpiece with red poinsettias and silver ribbons. I had little pinecones scattered on the perfectly pressed tablecloth. And I had Thomas the Tank Engine napkins.

Yes, I had forgotten to buy napkins. And not only that, but I had also inconveniently run out of plain white paper towels and dinner napkins. My lovely red cloth napkins were lost somewhere in the attic, and after forty-five minutes of looking on Christmas Eve, I gave up. So all I had were Thomas the Tank Engine napkins left over from Justen's birthday party.

And it was fine—really—but oh, what I would have done to have pretty little red napkins on my beautiful table.

Which is why today's project is for you to get your table settings for your holiday dinner planned out so everything is ready for the big event.

✳ **Project 20:** Get Your Table Stuff All Ready ✳

Today, I'm going to help you avoid the mad scramble on December 25 to find all the napkins, rings, tablecloths, and foof to make your dinner table look beautiful.

> ✳ ✳ ✳
>
> All you have to do is find all the stuff you need for your table setting right now so you have one less thing to fuss with on Christmas Day.

This project doesn't need a ton of explanation. All you really have to do is find all the stuff you need for your table setting right now so you have one less thing to fuss with on Christmas Day. So, set down your book and go and find:

✳ tablecloths (If they need ironing, you can be an over-achiever and iron them.)

✳ napkins

✳ table runners

✳ napkin rings

✳ Christmas plates

✳ silverware

If you are doing paper or plastic this year, write a list of what you will need so you can purchase those items way in advance and don't have to make a last-minute trip to the store (or use Thomas the Tank Engine napkins). Just be sure to recycle everything that you can in the gift wrap arena to lessen your paper impact on the planet.

Make It a Clutter-Free Christmas

Instead of hanging on to Christmas napkins for another eleven months, we use up any open packages of paper napkins, plates, or cups in January. Less clutter to deal with and store.

For our main dinner plates, I have twenty-four clear glass plates I bought ten years ago at IKEA for a buck each. They go with everything, look pretty on a table, and save on hassle. I use them for every holiday and any time we have more than eight people over for a meal. I have never regretted that purchase.

Kathi's Quick Tips

* If you see napkins, paper plates, or cups on sale, pick up extras.

* Use the same table settings each year. I know there is always something new and awesome on Pinterest, and I know it is so fun to change things up, but I suggest you get nice, basic stuff (a white tablecloth and red plates, for example) and then use your creativity with centerpieces and extras.

* Store all your table settings in one bin so they're easy to find and get out.

* Keep your table simple—the fun of the meal is togetherness, not fanciness.

* Add one new table decoration to your things each year. Last year, my mom made me a quilted table runner that looks great with my plates. This year, I plan to buy new napkin rings. That way, there's something fresh and new on your table without you spending a fortune.

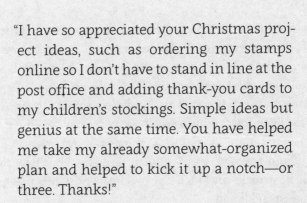

"I have so appreciated your Christmas project ideas, such as ordering my stamps online so I don't have to stand in line at the post office and adding thank-you cards to my children's stockings. Simple ideas but genius at the same time. You have helped me take my already somewhat-organized plan and helped to kick it up a notch—or three. Thanks!"

Beth

Your Personalized Special Project

For years, I have wanted to make my kids a tape of Christmas music. Back before iTunes playlists or even CD burners, we had to use one of those fancy dual cassette recorders (please say I'm not the only one who remembers these) to make new tapes.

Anyway, back when my kids were little, we used to blast Christmas music in my car during the holiday season. We all got very attached to certain songs, such as those on Bing Crosby's Christmas album (swoon), and I've often thought about how fun it would be to make my kids a tape of our favorite Christmas songs from their childhoods.

But I've never had the time, much less the technical wherewithal, to get it done. (Those dual cassette recordings were easy compared to iTunes.) But this year, since everything else is done early (thank you, Christmas projects), I decided to make this happen.

I had to recruit Roger's help, but I was able to put together a really cool playlist of favorite Christmas songs for each of my kids. Both of them were really excited to get it, and it felt so special to do something that was so...us.

✳✳✳

Think of your own special task that you have
wanted to do for years but have never had
time for. Today is your day to do that thing.

For your last project, I want you to think of your own special task that you have wanted to do for years but have never had time for. Maybe it's a tradition you want to start for your family, a surprise gift you want to pull off for one of your kids, or even a special holiday date night for your husband.

Today is your day to do that thing.

✳ ✳ ✳

✳ **Project 21**: Do that One Extra Special Thing ✳

I can't really tell you what to do for this project because I'm asking you to do something personal just for you and your family. But I do know that if you're like me, you probably want some ideas. So here are a few suggestions that might jumpstart your thinking as you begin this project.

Special Thing Ideas

* Plan a Christmas caroling outing. Go to neighbors' houses, knock on doors, and sing carols. Bring a plate of cookies for each stop.

* Make a special gift for your husband. Maybe it's those new cufflinks you've been eying on Pinterest or a special pancake mix in a jar you know he'd love.

* Make a special holiday dinner—not on Christmas but tonight. Maybe it's a holiday chili bar or a make-your-own pizza night coupled with a holiday movie marathon.

* Take your kids on a special Christmas outing. Go look at Christmas lights while you drink hot chocolate,

head to a Singing Christmas Tree performance, or go
window-shopping in the boutique section of town.

* Go to the bookstore and read Christmas books with
  your kids. Let them each pick a new one to buy.

* Have a holiday sleepover under the tree complete with
  a pillow fight.

Wrap-Up

And we're done!

Project 21 was the last Christmas project, which means you are not only done with all your Christmas stuff for this year, but it is now time to kick back with a mug of eggnog (or if you're like me, chai tea) and celebrate the season.

I have to just say it: I'm so proud of you. What an accomplishment!

Doesn't it feel great to have everything done, ready, *finito* so you can really enjoy these last few days of the holiday season with your family?

It feels great for me.

Merry Christmas!

✳ ✳ ✳

For those of you already thinking ahead to New Year's, I've put together the following bonus section, "The Five-Day Christmas Put Away," to get your house back in order and get ready to start the New Year.

The Five-Day Christmas
Put Away

I hope you had an amazing Christmas. Now that you've had some time to recuperate and clean up some wrapping paper, I want to give you an opportunity to pack up, clean up, and put away the trimmings so that next year, it will be drama free.

I'll walk you through a five-day put away starting whenever you're ready. I'll give you five days of instructions so that next year, you'll have a head start on everything Christmas.

When to take down your Christmas tree is a very personal decision. Bringing it up in mixed company (my husband and me) is sure to bring up issues in our marriage. Suffice to say, before we were married, my tree was down on December 26. We now leave it up until New Year's Day. Sigh.

So I'm going to leave it up to you to decide when to begin undecorating. I just want you to be prepared and ready to go when you do decide to pack it all away.

PROJECT 1

Take an Inventory

OK, we're keeping it simple today. All you have to do is take a quick inventory of what wrapping paper, ribbons, bows, and gift bags you have. You can also tally the number of paper plates, napkins, and cups you have, if your family uses them.

Then on your calendar for September or October (or whenever you get the itch to start stocking up), write down what you will need for next year.

Right now is also an excellent time to stock up. Plates on sale for 50 percent off? Bows on clearance? Time to stock up.

Do you need new Christmas lights for next year? A tree bag? Whatever you need, either get it or give your future self a clue and put it on your calendar!

PROJECT 2

Put Away the Paper

Today's task is to put away all the paper-related parts of the holiday. So where do you fall on the wrapping-paper scale?

1. "I always run out about December 20."

2. "Everyone in my family could come and wrap their gifts for the next five years, and I would still have enough paper left over to set up a wrapping stand at the mall."

3. "Doesn't matter. Every year I lay in a new supply on December 26!"

Wrap It Up

I am a box and ribbon saver. (So sue me.) I feel that I'm helping the environment, and it gives me a secret thrill to see how many times I can use the fluffy Santa bag before it looks trashy. The key to being able to reuse these items each year is to pack them up well.

> ✳ ✳ ✳
> The key to being able to reuse items each year is to pack them up well.

Before you destroy those sturdy boxes that all your presents were shipped in, keep the best of them to store your Christmas boxes, wrap, bags, tissue, and ribbon. I've even created some cute labels for you to print out and put on your boxes to make them easy to find next December. Go to ChristmasProject.org to download the free labels. You'll thank me next year.

Leave Notes to Your Future Self

* If you've purchased your Christmas cards this year (50 percent off!) for next year, put their exact location on your calendar (wall calendar, Outlook, Google Calendar) so you don't forget. I'd hate to have you buy more on December 15, only to find on December 20 the ones you bought last year.

* I put a note on my calendar for October 1 that reads, "Don't buy any Christmas wrapping paper. You have ENOUGH!"

* If you have to store your wrapping paper and bags in an out-of-the-way place (attic, basement), make a note of that on your calendar as well.

Put Away the Decor

Isn't it amazing how Christmas decor can take over every nook and cranny of your home?

I tend to spread my Christmas cheer over multiple rooms. I have some towels and soaps in the bathrooms, some snowman and log cabin dishes in the dining room, some winter-themed goblets in the kitchen, and table runners in the living room. Every year, I get everything packed up and put away on the highest shelf of the garage, only to discover that one of the wise men made a run for it and has been hiding out behind a throw pillow on the couch.

So today, go through *every* room and gather your Christmas wares. Here's a list of things with a Christmas theme to be on the lookout for:

* candles
* soaps
* tablecloths/table runners
* mugs
* dishes
* paper products
* ornaments
* kitchen towels
* napkins

* Christmas cards
* wrapping supplies
* stray decor

Get it all into one place. Ours usually hangs out on the kitchen table for a day or two. Make some decisions about what stays and what gets repurposed or recycled. Start a donation box of anything that hasn't made the cut in a couple of years and make space for the new treasures we all tend to collect.

Update Your Binder

Remember the three ghosts, Christmas Past, Christmas Present, and Christmas Yet to Come, in Charles Dickens's *A Christmas Carol*? If there was one thing your Christmas Present could tell your Christmas Yet to Come, what would it be?

"Remember the killer Rachael Ray roast-chicken recipe you tried this year? It was the bomb!" or "Everyone loved the reindeer cake pops on Christmas Eve. How about snowmen this next year?"

Well, that is precisely what your Christmas Binder is for.

> *** * ***
>
> Christmas Yet to Come will thank
> you when she doesn't have to hunt
> down the artichoke dip recipe.

Put all your favorite recipes, ideas, secret hiding places, and gift ideas for next year in your handy binder. Trust me, Christmas Yet to Come will thank you when she doesn't have to hunt down the artichoke dip recipe.

This is also the time to update that Christmas card list. Now! While you know where all those envelopes bearing return addresses are. Don't wait—seize the after-Christmas day!

Then make sure to put the binder someplace where you'll find it next year.

Returns and Exchanges

Did you buy too many Christmas lights (my husband would argue about whether that is possible)? Get a shirt in the wrong size? Do you have two friends who know you so well that they bought you the exact same book?

Don't let those things sit around your house until it's too late, and you end up just donating them to your favorite charity (which is preferable to hanging on to the item for three years and then donating it).

Get all your returns and exchanges together and take care of everything at once. You'll feel better once you have.

* * *

Whew! Don't you feel better? And even if you're not feeling the relief just yet, your future Christmas self will be so grateful that you cared enough about her to put away Christmas well this year.

Some of Our Family's
Favorite Recipes

⁜ Artichoke Dip ⁜

8 oz. cream cheese
1 cup Parmesan cheese, shredded
1 cup mayonnaise (low-fat or fat-free is acceptable)
½ tsp. dill weed
1 clove garlic, crushed
1 can artichoke hearts, drained and chopped

Preheat oven to 350°. Cream the cream cheese, add the Parmesan cheese, mayonnaise, dill weed, and garlic. Mix well. Fold in the chopped artichoke hearts and then spoon mixture into a 9 x 9 pan. Bake for 30 minutes. Serve with crackers, toasted baguettes, or toasted pita points. Serves 8 as an appetizer.

⁜ Goat Cheese Bruschetta ⁜

2 T. balsamic vinegar
2 T. extra virgin olive oil
2 T. chopped fresh herbs, such as dill, parsley, or basil
Toasted baguette
Goat cheese

Mix the balsamic vinegar, oil, and herbs together. Drizzle over slices of toasted baguette or other bread and spread with goat cheese. Finish with another drizzle of the vinegar-and-herb mixture. Garnish with a sprig of fresh thyme (optional).

✶ Drive-By Cheese Plate ✶

For those last-minute party invites. Just grab a plate and cheese knife from home. You can assemble once you arrive (or if you're like me, in the backseat of the car while your hubby is driving).

Grab at the store:

Camembert or other artisan cheese

Carr Table Water Crackers (or similar)

1 bunch of green grapes

✶ Roger's Pumpkin No-Bake Cheesecake ✶

16 oz. cream cheese

1 cup sugar

1 T. vanilla

1 T. lemon juice

¼ cup pumpkin pie filling

Premade graham cracker crust

Blend ingredients until creamy and fluffy. Pour into graham cracker crust. Garnish with cinnamon sugar (makes it look baked) and shaved white chocolate. Refrigerate for a few hours.

✶ Roger's Cranberry No-Bake Cheesecake ✶

16 oz. cream cheese

1 cup sugar

1 T. vanilla

1 T. lemon juice

1/3 cup whole cranberries in jelly

Premade graham cracker crust

Blend ingredients until creamy and fluffy. Pour into graham cracker crust. Garnish with any (or all) of the following: remaining whole cranberries/jelly (I put this just on the outside edge of the pie), orange peel zest, shaved white chocolate. Refrigerate for a few hours.

✳ Chocolate-Dipped Fruit ✳

1 11.5-oz. pkg. Nestle milk chocolate morsels
¼ cup vegetable shortening
Strawberries, grapes, bananas, apples, kiwi, or pineapple

In a double boiler, melt milk chocolate morsels and shortening over hot (not boiling) water; stir until smooth. Remove from heat but keep over hot water. (If chocolate thickens, return to heat; stir until smooth.) Dip pieces of fruit into chocolate; shake off excess. Place on foil-lined cookie sheets. Chill 10-15 minutes until chocolate is set. Peel off foil. Fruit may be kept at room temperature up to 1 hour. If chocolate becomes sticky, return to refrigerator.

✳ Kathi's Drunken Turkey ✳

1 gallon cold water
1 cup sea salt
1 T. crushed dried rosemary
1 T. dried sage
1 T. dried thyme
1 bottle dry white wine
3 oranges, cut in half
Turkey, defrosted

Directions

In a large clean garbage bag, combine all the ingredients.

Wash and dry your turkey. Make sure you have removed the innards. Place the turkey, breast down, into the brine in the bag. Make sure the cavity gets filled. Place the bag in a roasting pan and in the refrigerator overnight, turning once.

Remove the turkey carefully, drain off the excess brine, and pat dry. Discard excess brine.

Cook the turkey as desired, reserving the drippings for gravy. Keep in mind that brined turkeys cook 20 to 30 minutes faster, so watch the temperature gauge. Cook at 425° until a meat thermometer reaches 165°.

✳ Broccoli Casserole ✳

2 eggs, beaten
2 T green onions, chopped
1 can cream of celery soup
1 cup mayonnaise
2 10-oz. boxes frozen broccoli
8 oz. grated cheddar cheese
1 tube Ritz crackers
1 cube butter

Preheat the oven to 350°. Mix the first four ingredients in a bowl. Parboil broccoli and drain. Mix the broccoli into the first four ingredients. Pour into an 8x8 casserole dish. Sprinkle the cheese on top of the casserole. Melt the butter. Crush the tube of Ritz crackers and mix with the melted butter. Cover over the casserole. Bake for 30 minutes.

✳ Farmer's Breakfast Casserole ✳

2½ cups frozen hash brown potatoes or Tater Tots
¾ cup shredded Monterey Jack with (optional) jalapeno
    peppers
1 cup chopped fully cooked ham or Canadian bacon
    (optional)
¼ cup sliced green onion
4 eggs beaten or 1 cup egg substitute
1 12-oz. can evaporated milk (or 1½ cups evaporated
    skim milk)

¼ tsp. pepper
⅛ tsp. salt
1 pkg. Knorr Leek recipe mix
½ lb. asparagus or mushrooms, washed and cut into
    one-inch pieces
4 to 5 tomatoes, coarsely chopped

Spray a 2-quart square baking dish with cooking spray. Arrange potatoes evenly in the bottom of the dish. Sprinkle cheese, ham, green onion over all. In a mixing bowl combine eggs, milk, pepper, salt, leek recipe mix. Pour over mixture in baking dish. Sprinkle with Jane's Krazy Mixed-Up salt or Mrs. Dash (optional). Cover with foil or plastic wrap and refrigerate overnight. Next morning, bake uncovered at 350° for 30 minutes. Remove from oven; add asparagus or mushrooms and tomatoes. Bake for another 30 minutes until golden brown. Let stand 5 minutes before serving.

My Holiday Mission Statement

This is what I want Christmas to look like this year:

Dear Reader,

Thanks for being a part of *Get Yourself Organized for Christmas*. One of the greatest privileges I have is to hear back from the people who have used my books. I would love to stay in touch.

Website: www.KathiLipp.com
Facebook: facebook.com/authorkathilipp
Twitter: twitter.com/kathilipp
Mail: Kathi Lipp
171 Branham Lane
Suite 10-122
San Jose, CA 95136

In His Grace,

Kathi Lipp

Other books by Kathi Lipp

Clutter Free

If you've ever wished you could clear out your clutter, simplify your space, and take back your life, Kathi Lipp has just the solutions you need. Building off the success of her *The Get Yourself Organized Project,* this book will provide even more ideas for getting your life and your stuff under control.

Do any of these descriptions apply to you?

* You bought a box of cereal at the store, and then discovered you have several boxes at home that are already past the "best by" date.

* You bought a book and put it on your nightstand (right on top of ten others you've bought recently), but you have yet to open it.

* You keep hundreds of DVDs around even though you watch everything online now and aren't really sure where the remote for the DVD player is.

* You spend valuable time moving your piles around the house, but you can never find that piece of paper when you need it.

* Your house makes you depressed the moment you step into it.

As you try out the many easy, doable solutions that helped Kathi win her battle with clutter, you'll begin to understand why you hold on to the things you do, eliminate what's crowding out real life, and make room for the life of true abundance God wants for you.

The Get Yourself Organized Project

Finally, an organizational book for women who have given up trying to be Martha Stewart but still desire some semblance of order in their lives.

Most organizational books are written by and for people who are naturally structured and orderly. For the woman who is more ADD than type A, the advice sounds terrific but seldom works. These women are looking for help that takes into account their free-spirited outlook while providing tips and tricks they can easily follow to live a more organized life.

Kathi Lipp is just the author to address this need. In her inimitable style, she offers

* easy and effective ways you can restore peace to your everyday life

* simple and manageable long-term solutions for organizing any room in your home (and keeping it that way)

* a realistic way to de-stress a busy schedule

* strategies for efficient shopping, meal preparation, cleaning, and more

Full of helpful tips and abundant good humor, *The Get Yourself Organized Project* will enable you to spend your time living and enjoying life rather than organizing your sock drawer.

The Cure for the "Perfect" Life

12 Ways to Stop Trying Harder and Start Living Braver

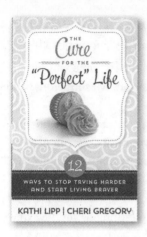

Are you crumbling under the burden of perfection? You know the expectations are unreasonable—even unreachable. And when everyone else seems more together than you, where do you turn for help?

Meet Kathi, a disguised perfectionist always looking to put everyone else's needs above her own, and Cheri, a formerly confused and exhausted poster girl for playing it safe. They've struggled just like you—and found the cure. With unabashed empathy and humor, they invite you to take part in their rebellion against perfection. Step-by-step they'll teach you how to challenge and change unhealthy beliefs. As they free you from always seeking more or needing approval of others, you'll discover a new, braver way of living. At last, you'll exchange outdated views of who you *should be* for a clearer vision of *who you are* in Christ.

The truth is you don't have to be perfect. You just have to be brave enough to read this book.

Happy Habits for Every Couple
21 Days to a Better Relationship

When was the last time you flirted with your husband? Was it before you had kids?

Do you spend more time on the couch with your wife watching movies or with a bag of chips watching The Game?

Does your idea of a hot date include a drive-thru and springing for the extra-large fries?

What would your marriage look like if for 21 days you turned your attention to happy habits that will better your relationship? Plenty of books describe how to improve a marriage, how to save a marriage, even how to ramp up intimacy in a marriage. In *Happy Habits for Every Couple*, Kathi Lipp and husband Roger show you practical, fun-filled ways to put love and laughter back into your marriage.

Here are just a few of the results you'll see when you put *Happy Habits for Every Couple* into practice:

* new levels of warmth and tenderness in your relationship

* a deeper sense of security with your spouse

* a marriage filled with fun and flirting

If you haven't given up the dream of being head-over-heels with your spouse again, following this 21-day plan will give you just the boost you need to bring you closer together.

The Husband Project

21 Days of Loving Your Man—on Purpose and with a Plan

Keeping your marriage healthy is all about the details—the daily actions and interactions in which you lift each other up and offer support, encouragement, and love. In *The Husband Project* you will discover fun and creative ways to bring back that lovin' feeling and remind your husband—and yourself—why you married in the first place.

Using the sense of humor that draws thousands of women a year to hear her speak, Kathi Lipp shows you through simple daily action plans how you can bring the fun back into your relationship even amidst your busy schedules.

The Husband Project is an indispensable resource that will help you to

* discover the unique plan God has for your marriage and your role as a wife

* create a plan to love your husband "on purpose"

* support and encourage other wives who want to make their marriage a priority

* experience release from the guilt of "not being enough"

If you desire to bring more joy into your marriage but just need a little help setting a plan into action, *The Husband Project* is for you.

21 Ways to Connect with Your Kids

You spend a good chunk of time making sure your kids are okay—they're getting good grades, doing their chores, and just enough cleaning that their rooms won't be condemned if the Board of Health happens to drop by. *21 Ways to Connect with Your Kids* offers a straightforward, workable plan that coaches you to do one simple thing each day for three weeks to connect with your kids.

Daily connection ideas include:

* planning a family fun night
* telling your child what you like about them
* developing a character growth chart
* writing a love note to your child
* working together on a family project

Written in Kathi's warm and personable but thought-provoking tone, this book will motivate you to incorporate great relationship habits into your daily life and give you confidence that you can connect with your kids even in the midst of busy schedules.